Praise for P

Dr. John Koessler puts his fing ......y spiritual life
with everything he writes. This book is a cool drink of water for
a thirsty soul. I don't need to be told to do more for God, I need
God's presence to help me live fully this day, this hour. Thank you,
Dr. Koessler.

CHRIS FABRY
Host of Chris Fabry Live

John Koessler's book *Practicing the Present* had me thinking about
my life and work from an angle I've almost never considered
before—the present. I'm constantly casting my eyes to the next
thing instead of living in the moment. This book helped me see
that I've often missed engaging God and others in the business
of the present. Pastoral work is so *daily* but it is difficult to make
the most of that reality. As I read, I wrote down several insights
that I need to work through in practice for the good of our church
and for my own good as well. Like me, you probably haven't read a
book with this focus before. There's no time like the present.

LEE ECLOV
Pastor, author, professor

It's a mistake to live *for* the moment. Most of us have figured that
much out. But few of us know how to live *in* the moment: fully
awake, utterly present, right here, right now. This moment is all the
time any of us ever gets, but it's so easy to squander it brooding
about the past or fretting about the future. Well, just in the nick
of time comes John Koessler's *Practicing the Present*. John is like
the rest of us, easily distracted. But unlike many of us—okay,
unlike me—he's mastering the art of inhabiting the moment—this
moment, right now—and of dwelling with the God who inhabits
it, too.

MARK BUCHANAN
Author of *The Rest of God* and *Godspeed: Walking as Spiritual
Formation*

Practicing the Present fluently drew me once again into discovery of God actively working in the present regardless of what I am experiencing. Seeing God's faithfulness in the past moves me to find God in the present alive, well, and active making my eyes to see and ears to hear Him as I live out my created purpose step-by-step in the present. It is so easy to be stuck in the past or the expectations of the future but Koessler shows from beginning to end that joy is found in the present moment. He shows how experiencing God fully in the present brings guidance in intuitive moments and brings us to our knees in worship and thanksgiving. To live in the present is to have a dynamic, transforming relationship with the one who loves us most.

JUDY TENELSHOF
Director of Spiritual Formation at Talbot

Practicing *the* Present

The Neglected Art of Living in the Now

John Koessler

MOODY PUBLISHERS
CHICAGO

All rights reserved. No part of this book may be reproduced in any form without permission in writing from the publisher, except in the case of brief quotations embodied in critical articles or reviews.

All Scripture quotations, unless otherwise indicated, are taken from the Holy Bible, New International Version®, NIV®. Copyright © 1973, 1978, 1984, 2011 by Biblica, Inc.™ Used by permission of Zondervan. All rights reserved worldwide. www.zondervan.com. The "NIV" and "New International Version" are trademarks registered in the United States Patent and Trademark Office by Biblica, Inc.™

Scripture quotations marked KJV are taken from the King James Version.

Published in association with the literary agency of Mark Sweeney & Associates, Bonita Springs, Florida.

Edited by Kevin P. Emmert
Interior and cover design: Erik M. Peterson
Cover photo of clock copyright © 2011 by RTimages / iStock (121031840).
All rights reserved.

Library of Congress Cataloging-in-Publication Data

Names: Koessler, John, 1953- author.
Title: Practicing the present : the neglected art of living in the now / John Koessler.
Description: Chicago : Moody Publishers, [2019] | Includes bibliographical references.
Identifiers: LCCN 2019003383 (print) | LCCN 2019010164 (ebook) | ISBN 9780802497413 () | ISBN 9780802418685
Subjects: LCSH: Awareness--Religious aspects--Christianity. | Mindfulness (Psychology) | Attention--Religious aspects--Christianity.
Classification: LCC BV4598.4 (ebook) | LCC BV4598.4 .K64 2019 (print) | DDC 248.4--dc23
LC record available at https://lccn.loc.gov/2019003383

ISBN: 978-0-8024-1868-5

All websites and phone numbers listed herein are accurate at the time of publication but may change in the future or cease to exist. The listing of website references and resources does not imply publisher endorsement of the site's entire contents. Groups and organizations are listed for informational purposes, and listing does not imply publisher endorsement of their activities.

We hope you enjoy this book from Moody Publishers. Our goal is to provide high-quality, thought-provoking books and products that connect truth to your real needs and challenges. For more information on other books and products written and produced from a biblical perspective, go to www.moodypublishers.com or write to:

Moody Publishers
820 N. LaSalle Boulevard
Chicago, IL 60610

1 3 5 7 9 10 8 6 4 2

Printed in the United States of America

For Al Errante,
old friend and fellow pilgrim.

Contents

Introduction

I'm a sucker for books and movies about time travel. *The Time Machine* by H. G. Wells, the time-traveling De-Lorean in *Back to the Future*, and any Star Trek episode in which the crew of the starship *Enterprise* travels back to the twentieth century—I love them all. But over the years, I've learned a few important things about time travel. For example, as far as I can tell from these books and movies, backward is better than forward. When you travel back in time, you know what you're getting. The future, on the other hand, is unknown and always seems to get worse. But that doesn't mean that the past is safe. When you travel back in time, you had better not touch anything. Apparently, the smallest change can have devastating effects on the space-time continuum. You may come back to the present and find that you don't exist.

In real life, I can't travel in time, but that doesn't mean I have no interest in either the past or the future. I'm often preoccupied with both. Sometimes it's because I'm thinking about the past, trying to understand what I have experienced and how it affects my life. Just as often I'm concerned about the future. I spent most of my youth preparing for a career that is now almost over. In my job as a college professor, I have spent twenty-five years equipping students for future ministry. As a Christian, my expectation is fixed on a hope that is yet to come. Like the patriarchs, I am longing for a better, heavenly country (Heb. 11:16).

What gets lost in all of this is the present. Like the quiet child in a loud family, it is often overlooked. You might think that this would not be the case. After all, aren't our immediate concerns always those of the present? What is more, between the past, present, and future, only the present is our constant companion. Despite this reality, there are many people who live in the past. For them, the present is merely the parade ground on which their personal history passes in review. Sometimes they are focused on the past because it seems preferable to the present. The past is where their golden age lies. They long for the "good old days" that will never come again. This shining vision of an era that probably never existed to begin with becomes the point of comparison for all the joys of the present. Not surprisingly, they all fall short of the mark. At other times, they may dwell on the past because they have been deeply scarred by it. They relive the trauma each time they think about it. Or they analyze the details of their past hoping to understand it.

Others are focused mainly on the future. They are not especially interested in the past. It seems like ancient history to them, as dusty as it is useless. Why dwell upon days that have gone by and will never come again? They would prefer to rush toward the future where all their dreams lie. These are people of vision. They usually don't concern themselves with the way things were, but only with how things might be in the future. If the present has value to them, it is only as a pivot point to the future. For future-oriented people, the present is easily left behind.

I understand both views. To some degree, they're both biblical. After all, the Bible has a lot to say about the past. The Bible begins with the story of creation, and many of its books are accounts of history. The Bible also has much to say about the future. Many of its books were written by prophets who foretold the future. The last book of the Bible concludes by painting us a picture of a world that does not yet exist. It casts our vision forward to the end of time, when the world we now know will be transformed into the world to come. Those who have followed the Bible's story line from the distant past to a distant future are left with a glorious vision of a new heaven and a new earth. This vision is reflected in some of the music we use in worship. One song declares, "This world is not my home, I'm just passing through."[1] Theologian N. T. Wright has observed that songs like this may inadvertently encourage a Gnostic attitude toward the present created world. "A massive assumption has been made in Western Christianity that the purpose of being a Christian is simply, or at least mainly, to 'go to heaven when you die,' and texts that don't say that but that mention heaven are read as if they did say it, and texts that say the opposite, like Romans 8:18–25 and Revelation 21–22 are simply screened out as if they didn't exist."[2] The hope of heaven is real. Scripture assures us that those who are absent from the body are present with the Lord (2 Cor.

5:8). But just as God has a purpose for the earth, He also has a purpose in the here and now (2 Cor. 5:9).

We sometimes brush by the present, as if it were some stranger that we pass on a busy street. Or if we do give attention to the present, it's usually only a kind of grudging consideration—the sort you might give to a smaller sibling who whines about a pressing need until your attention is wheedled away from the thing that really interests you. Someone has warned about the tyranny of the urgent. But what if it is not tyranny at all but instead a kind of temporal resentment? We ignore the present that is right in front of us until we have to take it seriously. When we are forced to do so, we become irritated.

Yet the same Bible that has a theology of history and a theology of the future also has a theology of the present. Frankly, it is easy to miss. Not because the Bible underemphasizes it, but because we have not been trained to see it. It has been said that familiarity breeds contempt, and few things are as familiar to us as the present. It is always there. The present is the only temporal space that we can inhabit. We can't recall it to mind because we haven't finished living through it. We can't really plan for it because it is unfolding in the moment.

Eugene Peterson talks about the importance of honoring time. He says that one of the most common ways that we desecrate creation is the profanation of time. What can he mean by this? We do not usually think about time in such terms. For us, time is merely a measure and a man-made measure to boot. Or else time is simply a commodity.

It is something that we buy or sell. Time is like money. It is a resource that we invest or squander. What Peterson suggests is radically reorienting because it means that time is more than a measure. It is also something more than a commodity to be bought, sold, or hoarded. Time is a gift of creation. It is not an accident of our material existence but a creation of God. As such, time is sacred. "Time is the medium in which we do all our living," Peterson explains. "When time is desecrated, life is desecrated."[3]

One of the most important implications of this is that time is where God meets us. If time is the medium in which we do all our living, then it is also the context within which all our interactions with God take place. As far as our experience is concerned, this is always in the present. When God meets us, He meets us in the here and now. Theologians and philosophers have taught us to think of God as being outside of time. Certainly, this is true as far as God's essential nature is concerned. God does not age. He is not bound by the limitations of time like we are. Yet as Creator, God not only created the medium in which we live our lives, but entered into it personally in bodily form. Jesus entered the same time-space reality that we inhabit. Not surprisingly, Jesus was acutely aware of time. He carried out His earthly ministry with a sense of the importance of timing. "My hour has not yet come," Jesus told His mother, when she pressed Him to reveal His divine power at the wedding in Cana (John 2:4). After members of His family responded to His messianic claims with contempt, Jesus repeated this statement: "My time is not yet here; for you any time will do" (John 7:6).

On the surface, this may sound like a dismissal of the present. It is really the opposite. It is clear that Jesus had a sense of the importance of the present moment. He knew where the present stood in relation to the past and the future, as well as the significance of its role in His ministry. To say that the time is not right does not mean that a particular moment is unimportant. I must have a clear sense of the significance of the present to know whether the time is right.

Eugene Peterson noted that our desecration of time is most often expressed in the forms of hurry and procrastination. "Hurry turns away from the gift of time in a compulsive grasping for abstractions that it can possess and control," he explains. "Procrastination is distracted from the gift of time in a lazy inattentiveness to the life of obedience and adoration by which we enter the 'fullness of time.'"[4]

In other words, hurry rushes toward the future with a callous disregard of both the past and the present. Procrastination moves in the other direction, either running away from the future, or at least dragging its feet, in a vain attempt to prevent its arrival. In both cases, the basic trajectory of time is clear. Time inevitably moves toward the future. Any understanding of how we should orient our lives to the past and the present must somehow be coordinated with the inevitability of the future.

In this book, I want to reorient our thinking, especially as leaders, to the present. Or more accurately, I want to help us reorient our thinking *in* the present. Leaders are biased toward the future. It is easy for them to miss the importance of the present. They are often largely responsible for creating a church culture that dismisses the significance of the here and now. My hope is that this book will help both leaders and those who are led by them to see the sacred value of the present.

To be sure, this is not a book about forgetting the past. Nor is it a book that will tell you to dismiss the future. It does not try to baptize the Buddhist practice that is sometimes called mindfulness by dressing it up in Sunday clothes and bringing it to church. This book is an exercise in biblical reflection that aims to put the present in its proper place—in both our thinking and practice. I have organized it by topics. Although the chapters are related, they do not really build upon one another. You might begin with chapter 1 or start with the chapter that focuses on the topic that interests you most. Although I try to make practical suggestions in every chapter, my discussion of specific practices or disciplines is concentrated in chapter 9.

In one sense, we cannot help but practice the present. We have no other temporal framework within which to live. Time travel is only the stuff of science fiction. We may remember the past, but we cannot return to it. We may place our hope in the future or dread its approach, but we cannot suddenly transport ourselves there. The present is the only context available to us for living out our lives. This book is not a call to favor the present over either the past or the future. It is an invitation to view our present circumstances, whatever they may be, through the lens of the sacred. We live our lives in the here and now. This is where we learn to obey God. The present is the place where we experience His presence.

———◦———

Chapter 1

Practicing the Present

I've reached the stage in life where it feels like I have more time behind me than in front of me. I know this isn't really true. I am a pilgrim wending my way toward a destination where time as I now experience it will have no meaning. I know this as a point of faith. But my day-to-day experience is something else. Where my ordinary life is concerned, it feels as if time is passing too quickly. I am like a driver who is running out of road, and it makes me wonder why I was in such a hurry to begin with.

An old hymn says, "Time, like an ever rolling stream, / Bears all its sons away." I know exactly what the hymn writer means. It is as if I am floating down a river, watching the trees along the bank. It is easy to think that I am the one who is stationary and everything else around me is moving. But I know better. Everything is in motion. The world in its present form is passing away, and so am I (see 1 Cor. 7:31).

For much of my life, I have been able to ignore this fact. Like most people, my interests and aspirations have been skewed toward the future. I have prayed for it, planned for it, and expended most of my effort trying to put it into effect. When I was not focusing on the future, I was dwelling on the past. Sometimes merely recalling it, more often brooding about it. In the process, I have learned an important lesson: the future never really arrives. The days marked on the calendar eventually do come to pass. The plans I make may come to fruition or else fail. Yet as far as my experience goes, I remain firmly rooted in the present. What is the future but the now that we have not yet come to know? Likewise, the past is merely a succession of presents that we have left behind.

My training as a leader taught me to focus mostly on the future. I thought my main goal should be to help the church become what it was not. Once our goals were met, I felt it was my job to find new goals and aim for those. Whatever we were doing could be done better. No matter how many were in attendance, we should always aim for more. More people, more programs, and more projects—I never felt as though we were quite what we should be. I thought I was "casting vision." Until one day, I read an article about the importance of saying thank you to the congregation and realized that most of my statements about the church from the pulpit tended to dwell on what we weren't doing. Instead of acknowledging what we were doing well, I usually pointed out our weaknesses. I thought I was being prophetic. The article helped me to realize that I was just being unappreciative.

Why was it so difficult for me to say thank you? It

was because I was disappointed. I thought my gifts were better suited for a different kind of church. I made it my mission to transform the congregation into the church I really wanted to serve. But when I started saying thank you, something changed. Not only did the church seem relieved, but I began to see the church differently. God was at work. People were growing in their faith. Certainly, there were areas where we could improve. But learning to say thank you helped me see what God was doing in the present.

Scattered in Time

It can be just as distracting to dwell on the past. If most church leaders have a bias toward the future, church members tend to look in the other direction. This is especially true of churches with a storied past. The longer the church's history, the greater the possibility that church members will view the present through the lens of what used to be. Usually, this takes the form of a narrative that is implicitly critical of the church that begins with the words, "I remember . . ." This vision of the past is bathed in golden hues, even when we are thinking of the trials that accompanied those days. That's because most of the sharp edges have been worn down by time and forgetfulness. The sermons were better in those days, the services fuller, and the church's ministries more effective.

The same thing can happen on a more personal level. We can become so absorbed with the past that it robs us of any pleasure that might come from the present. Maybe it's the memory of our own personal "glory days" that leaves us feeling that our life peaked years ago and it's all downhill from there. It could be the memory of a great mistake that fills us with so much regret that we carry the weight of it into the present. Or our minds may be fixed on some past trauma so that we live through it again and again in our memory.

Yet the more we reflect upon the past, the more illusory it becomes. That is because we are not merely recalling but recollecting. We sort through fragments of our past experiences the way an archeologist sifts the debris of an ancient civilization. Instead of bits of broken pottery, we handle shards of memory. These are not solid artifacts. They are ghosts, echoes of past perception. When we share them with others, we discover our perceptions do not always square with those of others. They remember things differently. Many times, these differences involve more than facts. They have to do with the experiences themselves. How is it possible that the same event that leaves me feeling so scarred years or even decades later was forgotten by others in a matter of minutes?

The future is equally illusive because it involves an imagined construction of a reality that does not yet exist. When God speaks of the future, we can be sure that it will come to pass. But when He does speak of it in Scripture, He usually does so by means of images and figures. Scripture offers a broad outline of what is to come and includes a few glimpses of that reality through the mist. But it never really provides us with a photograph or a detailed map. The Father's house has many rooms (John 14:2), but we do not know how they are decorated.

"I have been scattered in times I do not understand," St. Augustine complained. He saw his life as one that stretched in many directions at once. "My thoughts—the very inmost bowels of my soul—are torn to pieces in tumultuous vicissitudes, until that day when, purged and made liquid by the fire of Your love, I will flow into You."[1] The word that scholar Andrea Nightingale uses to characterize Augustine's view is "distended."[2] It is a good word because it conveys the notion that time is not only stretched between the past and the future, but also distorted.

Like Augustine's, our minds are scattered in time so that our interests range far beyond the present. At one moment, we peer intently into the past, hoping for the mists to clear and longing to catch a glimpse of a present that has disappeared from view. In the next, we skip far ahead, hoping to scout out the future and stake a certain claim. Unfortunately, the beauty and value of the present is often lost. We are here in body but not in mind. We are only halfhearted in our attention and sometimes in our service.

To the one whose interest is chiefly on the future, the present is only a way station. Its primary function is to serve as a staging ground for what comes next. For those whose focus is mostly on the past, the present becomes a cemetery filled with monuments to the glory days that will never come again or with a painful record of the injuries and slights we have suffered. For the future-oriented, the past is a drag and the present an obstacle. Either way, the present is where we are but not where we want to stay.

Interestingly, C. S. Lewis saw both perspectives as strategies of Satan, pointing out that humans live in time but are destined for eternity. God wants us to attend to both. But this can happen only if we understand the importance of the present moment, which Lewis calls "the point at which time touches eternity."[3]

Speaking in the voice of the master tempter Screwtape, Lewis observes,

> Of the present moment, and of it only, humans have an experience analogous to the experience which our Enemy has of reality as a whole; in it alone freedom and actuality are offered them. He would therefore have them continually concerned either with eternity (which means being concerned with Him) or with the Present—either meditating on their eternal union with, or separation from, Himself, or else obeying the present voice of conscience, bearing the present cross, receiving the present grace, giving thanks for the present pleasure.[4]

Lewis notes further that between these two, the future is the least like eternity: "It is the most completely temporal part of time—for the Past is frozen and no longer flows, and the Present is all lit up with eternal rays."[5]

The Trouble with the Future

Not so long ago, it was common for many churches to spend hours writing vision statements. Pastors and church boards labored to imagine a preferred future for their churches. That vision was captured in a sentence and pasted in the church bulletin. Some of us are still doing it. What is more, one person's vision of the future may reflect a different set of tastes, values, or expectations than another's. This is the fly in the ointment when it comes to ministry planning and what is often called "vision." What inspires pastors and church leaders is rarely what excites the average church member.

After several decades of reading these vision statements, I have come to three conclusions. First, they all sound pretty much the same. Church vision statements usually have something to do with worship, discipleship, and ensuring that people in the church are busy doing the church's work. They often employ hyperbolic language that promises more than the church actually delivers. Second, although their aim is to inspire, most vision statements are tedious in reality. My heart doesn't beat any faster when I read them. They don't make me say, "Yes, I want to be a part of that!" When I read them all I see is "blah, blah, blah, Jesus." Third, and perhaps most important, they are designed to create a culture of dissatisfaction with things as they are. The common assumption of these statements is that there is something deficient about the present. The future is where the real action is. The present is identified with the status quo, which is itself synonymous with stagnation and dead spirituality.

THE VISION THING

This is partly a reflection of context out of which vision statements arose. Vision statements did not really originate with the church, despite misguided appeals to the KJV translation of the first half of Proverbs 29:18: "Where there is no vision, the people perish." They come from the world of marketing. The mathematician and philosopher Archimedes is said to have declared, "Give me a lever long enough and a fulcrum on which to place it, and I shall move the world." The lever of the marketer is advertising and its fulcrum is dissatisfaction. Media critic Jean Kilbourne observes, "Advertising creates a world view that is based upon cynicism, dissatisfaction and craving."[6] General Motors executive Charles Kettering famously observed that the key to economic prosperity is "the organized creation of dissatisfaction."[7]

The basic message of the marketer is that we should *not* be content with what we have. You might think that the driving force in such an ethos would be satisfaction, but in reality, the opposite is true. Satisfaction has to do with one's needs. Robert and Edward Skidelsky explain the difference this way: "Needs—the objective requirements of a good and comfortable life—are finite in quantity, but wants, being purely psychic, are infinitely expandable, as to both quantity and quality."[8] Paul's list of necessities is shocking in its brevity. According to 1 Timothy 6:8, food and clothing are sufficient. Our wants are something else. They are the things we desire but can live without. The reason they are infinitely expandable is because they are easily replaceable. Once our wants are achieved, they soon give way to other wants. The aim of the marketer is to convince me that my wants are needs. Marketing is effective because it creates within me a sense of dissatisfaction and inflames my desire for what I do not have.

Pastors and church leaders who employ marketing techniques to further the church's mission do not buy into the cynicism and craving that lies behind the culture of advertising. Indeed, they would argue that their aim is to introduce people to the only One who is able to provide ultimate satisfaction. They may employ the methods of the marketer but they reject the bankrupt values of advertising culture. This is fair. But Neil Postman's warning about tools also holds true for strategies and methods. Postman observes that no tool is ideologically neutral: "In every tool is an ideological bias, a predisposition to construct the world as one thing rather than another, to value one thing over another, to amplify one sense or skill or attitude more loudly than another."[9] The bias of leadership that focuses primarily on an unrealized and preferred future is that that future is emphasized at the expense of the present. Suppose the vision we have set for the church becomes a reality? What then? We will likely feel compelled to formulate a new vision. In other words, the vision itself really doesn't matter. It is merely the carrot at the end of the stick that keeps us in motion. The result is an endless missional treadmill. We do not really expect to achieve our goal. Or if we do achieve it, we simply replace it with another goal. The main thing is to be fixed on the future and move toward it.

THE TREADMILL OF DESIRE

A vision can be a help when we are setting goals but it can also be a trap. Proverbs 27:20 warns, "Death and Destruction are never satisfied, and neither are human eyes." Ambition, like human desire, seems to be infinitely expandable. Once we have reached our goal, it is immediately replaced with another. At its best, ambition provides the energy we need to improve and accomplish. At its worst, it becomes an endless treadmill that only proves that we will never be satisfied no matter how much success we experience.

While ambition and desire are not automatically incompatible with the Christian life, they only concentrate our attention on what we lack. The first and fourth beatitude remind us that this is not necessarily a bad thing (Matt. 5:3, 6). But the Bible also counsels us to pursue contentment, noting that "godliness with contentment is great gain" (1 Tim. 6:6).

The church that is focused on some golden age in the past has a similar problem. But in this case, the church's attention is twice divided. It dwells on a past that will never return while at the same time trying to move toward a future that looks like the past. There is twice the incentive to dismiss the work that God is doing in the here and now. If we see His work, we are liable to scorn it. We become like those who wept when they compared the smaller second temple that was rebuilt in the days of Ezra and Nehemiah to the glory days of the temple of Solomon. Haggai 2:3 captures their disappointment: "Who of you is left who saw this house in its former glory? How does it look to you now? Does it not seem to you like nothing?"

Whether we are focused on a future that never quite becomes a reality or are longing for a treasured past that will not return, the effect on our view of the present is the same. Both perspectives tend to marginalize the present. The present seems like nothing to us. I suppose we should not be surprised by this truth. The Christian faith has a vested interest in the future. The return of Christ is in the future. The ultimate fulfillment of all His promises about the kingdom will take place in the future. Our resurrection and final deliverance from our struggle with sin remains in the future. It is true that where the Christian is concerned the best is yet to come. Likewise our Christian faith has deep roots in the past. Our hope is grounded upon promises made long before we were born. The Bible on which we have staked our faith and our lives was written by and addressed to people who are now long dead. That same

Bible admonishes us to remember what we have received and heard, as well as to remember those who have believed before us (see Rev. 3:3; Heb. 13:7). Remembering is a fundamental discipline of the Christian life, and the primary reference point for those who remember is the past.

Paul's determination to forget what is behind and strain toward what is ahead expressed in Philippians 3:13 seems to favor the future over both the past and the present. His admonition to the Ephesians that they should remember that they were once Gentiles separated from Christ and to the Thessalonians that they should recall what he was like when he was with them both show that he had a regard for the past (Eph. 2:11; 1 Thess. 2:9). Jesus said that the God of Abraham, Isaac, and Jacob "is not the God of the dead, but of the living" (Luke 20:38). This makes Him the God of our past and of our future as much as He is the God of our present. He is the one who has promised and called in the past. His grace is the remedy for all our regret. His assurances are our guarantee and our hope for the future. But our experience with Him is always in the present.

God's ultimate purpose for us lies in the future, but His business with us is always in the present. He has left us a record of His faithfulness in the past, but that is so we can be confident of His dealings with us in the here and now. Satan's strategy is to distract us from the divine present by directing our attention either to a past that we can no longer effect or to a future that does not yet exist and may never come to pass. This may take the form of a dogged pursuit of the future, which leaves us blinded to or dissatisfied with the present. Or it may be an obsession with the past, whether it is a longing for the glory days or an overwhelming sense of regret over decisions, actions, and experiences that we now cannot change. Each of these perspectives makes us vulnerable to the same error made by the people of Haggai's day. Either we will not see what God is doing in the present or we will note it and dismiss it as "nothing."

Practicing the Present

In this book, I propose an alternative. I call it "practicing the present." Practicing the present involves more than the habit of slowing down and making ourselves aware of what is going on in the moment. It is a way of locating ourselves in the world. It is a way of seeing. Practicing the present has Christian roots. Jesus warned His disciples, "Therefore do not worry about tomorrow, for tomorrow will worry about itself. Each day has enough trouble of its own" (Matt. 6:34). He taught us to ask the Father for our "daily" bread (Matt. 6:11). Jesus does not mean that we should ignore the future. But He does warn against the danger of being consumed with it. James has similar advice for those who are overconfident about the future: "Now listen, you who say, 'Today or tomorrow we will go to this or that city, spend a year there, carry on business and make money,'" he warns. "Why, you do not even know what will happen tomorrow. What is your life? You are a mist that appears for a little while and then vanishes" (4:13–14).

In his book *Beginning to Pray*, Anthony Bloom notes that one of the things we must learn to do if we are to pray well is to "establish ourselves in the present."[10] Bloom describes a process that helps beginners at prayer to orient themselves to the present. Bloom explains, "You sit down and say, 'I am seated, I am doing nothing, I will do nothing for five minutes,' and then relax, and continually throughout this time (one or two minutes is the most you will be able to endure to begin with) realise, 'I am here in the presence of God, in my own presence and in the presence of all the furniture that is around me, just still, moving nowhere.'"[11] This is an act in which we concentrate our attention both on the moment and on our immediate surroundings. We become aware of our senses. But more than that, we remind ourselves of the reality of God's immediacy and His presence. You might think this would be easier to do in a digital age. After all, don't our smartphones provide us with continual reminders to pay attention to the immediate? In reality, they often draw our attention away from our surroundings and those who are in them. How often have we seen two people seated in close proximity but ignoring each other while their faces are glued to a glowing screen? Worst of all, these devices make it difficult to concentrate on God's presence. They demand our immediate attention but hinder us from focusing on living in the present.

Bloom learned the importance of living in the present when he was fighting with the resistance movement in German-occupied France during World War II. He was caught by the police and realized that his life was in jeopardy. Two things happened in that moment. First, he suddenly became very aware of the present. "For one thing, I began to think very quickly, feel very intensely, and to be aware of the whole situation with a relief and a colourfulness which I had never before perceived on the last steps of Metro Etoile."[12] Second, Bloom realized that he could not think about the past. He couldn't talk about his real past without being shot. The past he was prepared to talk about did not really exist. "I discovered that I was pressed into the present moment, and all my past, that is, all the things that could be, were condensed in the present moment with an intensity, a colourfulness that was extremely exhilarating and which allowed me eventually to get away!"[13]

People who live through a traumatic experience sometimes say that it is like an "out of body experience." But what Bloom describes sounds more like the opposite. Maybe what is really going on is that we are shocked out of our concerns about the past and the future and are suddenly fully absorbed in the present.

Those who practice the present try to do something similar but within the context of ordinary life. Instead of waiting for someone to put a gun to our head, we develop the habit of reining in our wandering mind and concentrating our attention on the present. This means, first of all, taking stock of things as they really are. What is the real landscape of my life? What do things really look like? We are doing more than assessing. We are trying to orient ourselves to reality. Those who dwell on the past and future are often living in a fantasy world. But God is at work in the real world. As we take stock of things as they really are, we do so with an awareness that God is truly present no matter how mundane or how bleak the circumstances appear.

Consequently, we are looking for the evidence of God's presence in the present. Pastor and theologian Helmut Thielicke observed that Jesus Christ "always lingers in the darkest places in the world."[14] But Jesus is equally present in the common places. Jesus was "a man of suffering, and familiar with pain" (Isa. 53:3). Yet He was also acquainted with the mundane. If the silence of the Bible is any indication, the bulk of Jesus' earthly life was spent living an ordinary life. Most of His first thirty years were spent living the same kind of life that anyone else might have lived. Jesus lived with His parents (Luke 2:51). He grew up in the village they called home. He learned a trade.

Those who practice the present take note of the fact that God dwells in the midst of the muck and mire of daily life. Just as Anthony Bloom taught those who are learning to pray to acknowledge that God is present in the room along with the furniture, those who practice the present must recognize God's presence in their circumstances just as they are. They must accept that they are "just still, moving nowhere." The aim is not to look for a solution to our problems or to position ourselves for future success. It is, as Psalm 46:10 says, to "be still, and know that I am God." This is a habit of self-reminder, not a feeling. We do not have to experience a sense of God's presence in order for it to be true. Yet once we acknowledge the reality of His presence, we are more likely to become aware of it.

Practicing the present does not ignore the future or the past. But it does view both with a measure of sanctified skepticism. Both can be an unhealthy refuge for those who are disappointed with their present. Practicing the present also demands that we rein in, as much as we are able, our ambition and our anxiety. Both are common to human experience, and each in their own way can blind us to the reality of God's presence. They can cause us to forget the One who has numbered the hairs of our head and who is really responsible for the effectiveness of what we do for Jesus. Both ambition and anxiety can cause us to take too much responsibility for the success or the failure of what we do. Like Paul, we must refuse to judge ourselves (1 Cor. 4:3). When we are tempted to draw conclusions about what we see, we remind ourselves that our location in the present does not give us enough perspective to accurately weigh what we have done. When the Lord comes, "He will bring to light what is hidden in darkness and will expose the motives of the heart. At that time each will receive their praise from God" (1 Cor. 4:5).

In his memoir *Open Secrets*, Richard Lischer describes his experience as pastor of a small rural church in central Illinois. One night during his first week, the phone rang at three o'clock in the morning. The parishioner on the other end was a man named Ed whose wife Doral's gallbladder had ruptured. "It ain't good. It ain't good at all," he told Lischer. "We're goin' to have surgery in thirty, forty minutes. We need you here—if you can."[15] Lischer dressed quickly in his clerical garb and rushed along back roads through the darkness to the hospital. He found Ed and Doral waiting in a laundry alcove next to the operating room. "I wasn't sure what was expected of me," Lischer writes. "If there was a ritual for this sort of situation, I didn't know it."[16]

At first, the three just stood huddled together in fear and silence. At a loss for words of his own, Lischer turned to the familiar script of the liturgy. "The Lord be with you," he said. "And with thy spirit," Ed and Doral replied in unison. "Lift up your hearts," Lischer said. "We lift them to the Lord," they answered.

There, in the dim light of the alcove, God showed up. "The Lord assumed his rightful place as Lord of the Alcove, and the three of us wordlessly acknowledged the presence," Lischer writes. "That night the Spirit moved like a gentle breeze among us and created something ineffable and real."[17]

This seems to me to be a perfect example of life and ministry in the present tense. It is a matter of acknowledging the reality of God's presence in the rough-and-tumble of ordinary ministry. It is a matter of expecting God to show up, even in the fear and boredom of the hospital waiting room. It is the honest acceptance that, at least in some measure, the past is lost to us and the future is unattainable. I do not mean that time does not exist or that it does not matter. It does. We are moving through time. Yet as we make this journey, God is moving with us. He is always with us, and we are only ever in the present with Him.

Chapter 2

Take No Thought

A few years ago, I was diagnosed with cancer. Although it was a common form that is often treatable, I was shattered by the news. I felt betrayed, not so much by God, but by my own body. I lay awake nights thinking about the thing I had inside me and wishing that I could go back to the day before I knew of the diagnosis. When the doctor told me that my surgery appeared to be successful, I felt like a condemned prisoner who has just been given a pardon. "This is what forgiveness feels like," I told my wife.

Five years after the surgery, my blood work showed a slight change, and I panicked. The doctor assured me that the difference was insignificant. As far as he was concerned, I was still cancer free. Yet the old fear had returned, and I found it difficult to break free from it. What if the doctor was wrong? How did I know that the next test results wouldn't show that my cancer had come back? I still think about it.

Fear often casts a shadow over the future as we worry about things that might happen. We also fret about the past. Sometimes we worry that we have taken a wrong turn along the way or we regret some choice we have made. We wonder how the past has shaped our present or how it will affect our future. We speculate about how things might be different if we had acted otherwise. The trouble with all such fears is that we can do nothing about them. Once our choices have been made and the action is taken, we cannot go back and undo them. No matter how much we may regret the past, we do not have the power to change it. The future is similarly out of reach. We can speculate but we cannot know for certain what the future will be like. The past is a shadow, and the future a mirage. Scriptures tell us to be wary of both.

Jesus warned of the danger of dwelling on the past when He said that one who puts his hand to the plow and "looks back" is not fit for service in the kingdom of God (Luke 9:62). He likewise cautioned His disciples not to fret about the future: "Therefore do not worry about tomorrow, for tomorrow will worry about itself. Each day has enough trouble of its own" (Matt. 6:34). According to the KJV rendering, we are to take "no thought for the morrow."

These words are comforting, until we begin to actually think about them. How can we avoid thinking about tomorrow? Is Jesus even being realistic when He asks this of us? What is more, despite these words, the Gospels make it clear that Jesus Himself gave thought to both the past and the future. Jesus remembered the glory He had before the incarnation (John 17:5). He asked the Father to remove the cup of suffering He was about to experience (Matt.

26:38–39). If Jesus thought about the past and the future, why would He expect us to do otherwise?

God of the Here and Now

The answer is that He does not. Jesus does not counsel us to ignore the future, despite the way the KJV translators rendered Matthew 6:34. The admonition to take "no thought for the morrow" is really an encouragement to practice the present. Jesus urges us to shift the focus of our attention from the uncertain future to the certainty of God's presence in the here and now. Wherever we may be headed in days to come, we will not be going there alone. Jesus tells us to stop imagining what might happen and open our eyes to what is going on around us. "Look at the birds of the air," He says. "See how the flowers of the field grow" (vv. 26, 28).

It is tempting to treat these words as merely a poetic flourish. They are lovely but impractical. Thielicke observed, "All the idyllic pictures in this text of carefree birds and happy lilies and the glory and splendour of Solomon cannot hide from us the fact that Jesus is saying something tremendously upsetting here; upsetting simply because now it all has to be transposed from the light of nature into drab grey of our everyday life."[1] For some, Jesus' commands on this matter sound suspiciously like denial.

But what if we viewed them differently? Suppose we treated them the way we might the observations of a naturalist. Jesus is not asking us to close our eyes but to open them and observe how things actually work here in the real world. According to Jesus, God provides for what He has created, even the most insignificant. In Matthew 7:9–11, Jesus further invites us to look at the circumstances through the eyes of an anthropologist. "Which of you, if your son asks for bread, will give him a stone? Or if he asks for a fish, will give him a snake?" Jesus asks. "If you, then, though you are evil, know how to give good gifts to your children, how much more will your Father in heaven give good gifts to those who ask him!"

There is a profound irony in this statement. It suggests that we expect more of ourselves than we do of God. We thought that our anxiety about the future was a function of our realism. We were simply trying to anticipate what might happen in order to prepare for the worst. Jesus judges our vision to be a fantasy. It is a fantasy of dread, to be sure, but a fantasy nonetheless.

Does Jesus think that what is to come will be all hearts and flowers? Is He only another huckster who plays on our fears and tells us to engage in positive thinking? Or worse, is He merely a naïve spiritual leader who counsels us to take the path of denial by telling us that as long as we expect good things we will get good things? Neither of these views seems consistent with the portrait of Christ that we find in the New Testament or with His own words. It is Jesus who is the realist, and we are the ones who do not have a grip on reality.

Likewise, Jesus does not tell us to forget about the past. His plan for dealing with our fear of the future is not to develop amnesia. Just the opposite. Our answer to the Savior's questions about a child's request for bread or fish depends upon a shared common experience. This is an experience not only of ordinary human affection but of God. Either way, it is an argument from the past that anchors us to the present. Whatever we have to deal with in the present, we are not asked to face it as spiritual orphans. Your Father in heaven not only hears your request, but also knows what you need before you ask Him (Matt. 6:8).

Putting the Past Behind Us

The future is not the only thing that keeps us from living in the present tense. For many, thinking about the past makes us just as anxious as worrying about the future. God redeems our past but He does not change it. God causes all things to work together for the believer's good (Rom. 8:28). But this doesn't mean that everything that has happened to us is good. It certainly doesn't mean that everything we have done is good. For some, it is not a fear of the future but the recollection of the past that is the chief stumbling block in their life. We are living with what Martyn Lloyd-Jones calls "vain" regret. This is the condition of those whose past actions have crippled them in the present. "You cannot look back across your past life without seeing things to regret," Lloyd-Jones warns. "That is as it should be; but it is just there that the subtlety of this condition comes in and we cross that fine line of distinction that lies between a legitimate regret and a wrong condition of misery and of deception."[2]

HAUNTED BY THE PAST

You don't have to believe in ghosts to be haunted. Many of us are haunted by the past. Is there anything we can do when we feel anxious about things that have already happened? Here are three ways of dealing with troubling thoughts about the past:

- *Talk to somebody about it.* Often we are haunted by the memory of things we have never shared with anyone else. It may be a traumatic experience or an action that now makes us feel ashamed. It can be helpful to tell a pastor, counselor, or friend.

- *Write about it.* Anxiety has a tendency to keep us from focusing. We do not think clearly so that our assessment of the situation is out of proportion with the events themselves. Writing about it can help us focus our thoughts and assess things more realistically. Consider keeping a journal.

- *Forget about it.* C. S. Lewis once said that one of the functions of faith is to tell your moods "where they get off."[3] Sometimes, the best thing we can do is to turn over and go to sleep. We cannot change the past. We are haunted by things over which we had no control. Accept your powerlessness and hand the whole situation over to God. Pray this prayer: "God, I am giving this to You. This is Your problem now."

It is not regret itself that is the problem but empty regret that falls short of true repentance and does not take into account the forgiveness of Christ. Regret is not always a sign of repentance. Esau regretted selling his birthright to Jacob for a bowl of lentil stew but his regret fell short of true repentance (Heb. 12:16–17). Judas regretted handing Christ over to the Romans for the chief priests and elders. He was so overcome with remorse that he felt he could not go on living (Matt. 27:3–5). What distinguished his remorse from the kind of regret that the Bible calls repentance? In both cases, the problem was an incomplete regret. In Esau's case, his regret appears to have been limited to the consequences of his decision but not to the decision itself. He regretted the loss of his inheritance but failed to grieve over his own part in the loss. As far as Esau was concerned, the fault lay with Jacob (Gen. 27:36). But according to Hebrews 12:16, the root of the problem could be traced to Esau's spiritual values—or rather, the absence of them.

Esau valued the benefits that came with his father's blessing but had no regard for their spiritual significance. He was profane. His remorse is a sobering reminder that it is possible to regret the consequences of an action or even the action itself and yet still have no regard for God.

Judas's remorse was just as profane, but in a very different way. Esau felt remorse over what he had thrown away, but Judas regretted what he had gained. The turning point for Judas appears to have been the recognition that Jesus was condemned as a result of his betrayal (Matt. 27:3). The betrayer admitted his guilt and attempted to rid himself of its reward. In Matthew 26:24, Jesus warned, "The Son of Man will go just as it is written about him. But woe to that man who betrays the Son of Man! It would be better for him if he had not been born." It was Judas's final act that ultimately exposed the profane nature of his repentance. His was a remorse that did not include a vision of God's grace or of Christ's forgiveness. If anything, Judas's behavior seems to be an attempt to atone for his own sins. True repentance involves regret, but it is not enough to feel bad. Regret that does not also hold in view the hope of forgiveness through Christ will only lead to despair. This is what Paul meant when he distinguished between a "repentance that leads to salvation and leaves no regret" from the kind of "worldly sorrow" that "brings death" (2 Cor. 7:10). God is not mainly interested in making us feel bad about our past. What does He gain from our grief? The remorse that we feel in true repentance motivates us to turn from our sin and receive the embrace of Christ.

For pastors and church leaders, this kind of regret is further complicated by the fact that many of the consequences we must deal with come from choices others make. They are beyond our control. We lead in an environment that was shaped by the actions of those who were there before we arrived on the scene. We are trying to clean up a mess that we did not make. Maybe we have tried to cast a vision for a better future for the church, but the congregation has not embraced it. Church members come to us for counseling about foolish or sinful actions they have committed in the past and expect us to fix their problem in a thirty-minute session.

Living in the Present Tense

Practicing the present is not a flight from reality. Jesus does not teach us to dismiss the past or ignore the future. Practicing the present is not the habit of looking at our lives through the rose-colored glasses of sentimentality. Neither is it a careless disregard of the things that need to be done to prepare for the future. Instead, it is the practice of orienting ourselves to the present because it is in the present that the past and the future meet. The only way to deal with the past is to attend to the concerns of the present. Likewise the present is the foundation upon which the future is built. As C. S. Lewis observes, "The duty of planning the morrow's work is *today's* duty; though its material is borrowed from the future, the duty, like all duties, is in the Present."[4]

Sentimentalism recasts the past, smoothing out its sharp edges and minimizing the damage done. The cynic may view history with a jaundiced eye, but the sentimentalist rewrites it in a way that obscures the sin and pain. When Israel longed for the fleshpots of Egypt, they viewed their recent history through the lens of sentimentality (Ex. 16:3).

They remembered the food but forgot their own desperate cries for God's deliverance (Ex. 2:23).

Spiritual sentimentalism also distorts our view of the future. It does this by the same means it employs to skew our vision of the past. Sentimentalism minimizes the hardships that come with the future and overestimates the benefits that are to be found there. This airbrushed vision of what our lives should be like does not correspond to any experience we have actually had. It is often a false vision of the "good old days" projected into the future. Such a vision is unattainable. We cannot go back there because we were never from there. The pots of meat were never that full. The garlic and leeks that we long to eat did not taste as good as all that, and they were far more expensive than we remember (Num. 11:5).

God offers believers a certain hope for the future. But He does not necessarily promise that our path to the future will be a smooth one. When Paul and Barnabas travelled through Lystra, Iconium, and Antioch strengthening the disciples, their strategy for encouraging the church was to paint a realistic view of their future. The essence of their message was: "We must go through many hardships to enter the kingdom of God" (Acts 14:22). One wonders whether today's preachers would have the courage to do the same. Indeed, one wonders whether many of today's preachers even believe the same gospel as Paul. If we could we would prefer to exclude hardship from our vision of the future. Practicing the present involves a commitment on our part to resist our natural inclination toward sentimentalism. It demands an unflinching commitment to truth as the Bible defines it. This is one of Scripture's main functions, to help us interpret our experience realistically as God defines reality.

For pastors and church leaders, this begins with a recognition that reality as the Bible defines it is one that has been affected by sin. God has not called us to serve our fantasy church but one that exists in the real world. It is the broken church filled with failure and disappointments that He has chosen to be the instrument of His grace. A necessary corollary to this truth is our recognition that the broken world in which we live and do ministry is one that is leaning into redemption. As Romans 8:19 says, creation "waits in eager expectation for the children of God to be revealed." The broken landscape of the present is one where we can expect to meet God. It is also one that God has promised to reclaim. Our hope is in the future, but the present is the field of God's activity.

Those who practice the present must be intentional about living life in the present tense. We might wonder whether we have the option to do otherwise. We are not time travelers. We cannot visit the past or project ourselves into the future. But while we live in the present, we do not always attend to the present. Our minds are occupied elsewhere. We spend our days living in the present but ranging in our thinking from the past to the future. Meanwhile, the swiftly passing present is squandered. How, then, do we live in the present tense? One of the most important ways we do this is by focusing on the task at hand. We attend to what has been set before us. The task at hand is not glorious. For pastors and leaders, it is the basic work of shepherding. Shepherding involves keeping watch over yourself and the flock God has called you to serve (Acts 20:28).

Jesus characterizes the present as a realm where we must exercise faith when He says that each day has enough trouble of its own (Matt. 6:34). This is both a forceful reminder of our powerlessness and a call to attend to our duty. "Can any one of you by worrying add a single hour to your life?" Jesus asks in Matthew 6:27. Has worry ever protected us from such things in the past? Most of our worries are about things over which we have no control. Many of them will never even come to pass. Yet knowing this does not rescue us from anxiety. The power of worry is its ability to play upon our uncertainty.

Our Double Delusion

According to Jesus, we are suffering from a double delusion. First, our anxiety about the future is grounded in a false assumption about who is actually in control. We think we are in control, but we are not. We do not even control the most basic elements of our own life and environment. We can take measures to guard our health, but we cannot add to the length of our days. We can make provision for our future, but we cannot stop moth and rust from corrupting what we possess or guarantee that thieves will not carry it off. Today's troubles are proof enough that we cannot build a wall strong enough to keep them out.

Second, our fears reflect a secret suspicion that the God who should be in control is actually asleep at the wheel. We are afraid that God is not as attentive to our situation as He should be. Consequently, we attempt to wrest control from God by taking matters into our own hands. We rely on our own strategies more than upon God, depending on the flesh rather than the Spirit. In our eagerness to produce results, we resort to questionable methods. Worse yet, we may adopt methods that fall outside the bounds of what Scripture says is wise or even allowable. In ministry, this kind of anxiety often takes the form of unreflective pragmatism. We focus on results without considering whether the measures we take to achieve them are responsible or biblical. We assume the end justifies the means. Another way in which leaders often react when they fear that God is not attentive is by resorting to manipulation. We rely on our own persuasive techniques to move people to act rather than waiting for the Holy Spirit to convict.

It's easy to see why we might be deluded into such thinking. The universe is large, and we are small. God is great, and we are mostly concerned about trivial matters. They are not trivial to us, but if we compare the things that trouble us to the great concerns of the world, our deepest concerns often seem petty. It is all too easy to believe that we are lost in the crowd. In other words, the root of our anxiety does not really lie in our circumstances but in our souls. The fear we feel is evidence of our lack of faith. We thought that the solution was to change our temporal location either by taking refuge in the past or hurrying into the future. Instead, the answer is to remain firmly rooted in the present and to look for God.

By saying that today has enough trouble of its own, Jesus reminds us that all these things we have been trying to avoid have come to us by divine appointment and we are called to be faithful in them. Whatever was true of the past and whatever may come to pass in the future, we have enough to occupy us in the here and now. Yet why would Jesus think that these vivid reminders of our impotence bring any comfort? The reality check that He provides may be alarming at first because it underscores our helplessness and vulnerability, but once we have recovered from the shock, it comes to us as something of a relief. It turns out we have been trying to shoulder a burden we were never meant to carry. What our anxiety about the future really amounts to is a failed attempt to put ourselves in the place of God. We have been trying to control our own destiny.

Church leaders are especially vulnerable to this. Those who serve God sometimes develop a God complex. We think we can accomplish more than is really possible. We demand that God do His work according to our timetable. We replace God's agenda with priorities of our own. Our desire to be in control causes us to focus our attention on systems, programs, and methods rather than on people in an effort to advance our interests. Of course, in our minds the aim of good systems and methods is to serve people. We do not believe that we are being selfish by devoting ourselves to such things. "When my leadership was more event or program focused I would have said that everything

I was doing did serve people," Alan Fadling observes. Upon more mature reflection, Fadling realized that those efforts were only indirectly for people. "Most of my energy and focus were on making the *things* better rather than serving *people* better."[5]

The distinction that Fadling makes is subtle and important. Ministry methods and organizational systems are not inherently evil. But even divinely ordained systems can be subverted for selfish purposes. This was Jesus' point when He warned that the Sabbath was made for man, and not man for the Sabbath (Mark 2:27).

The Sacred Value of Ordinary Life

This means that to live in the present tense, we need to recognize the sacred value of ordinary life along with all the problems that attend it. Those who practice the present sanctify the commonplace. Anxiety isn't the only thing that keeps us from focusing on the present, sometimes its boredom. The things that are of immediate concern aren't very interesting to us. They don't seem significant enough, especially if we are trying to make a mark for ourselves. We do not dream of church board meetings but of invitations to speak at conferences, to write books, and what is euphemistically called "a larger field of opportunity" but would be more accurately described as a promotion. We keep track of church attendance not because we want to know who might need a pastoral visit but so that we can take pleasure in our own success. The daily duties of prayer, sermon preparation, discipleship, and hospital visitation seem less attractive to us than our vision of what our future ministry success will look like.

Eugene Peterson has labeled such fantasies as ecclesiastical pornography and warns, "All such fantasizing withdraws energy from the realities at hand and leaves us petulant."[6] This way of thinking also makes it impossible for us to show the congregation the sacred value of their jobs, their families, and the daily tasks of ordinary life. We cannot convey this truth to them because we do not really believe it ourselves.

During the Reformation, Martin Luther challenged the common worldview that separated callings into secular and sacred. For Luther, service to God was not only the province of clergy, it was the responsibility of all who had been called into a relationship with Christ. Each one serves God in the context in which he or she finds himself. The butcher, baker, servant, and soldier serve God by serving the community in their work just as the clergy did by serving the community through the offices of the church. In other words, Luther recaptured the biblical sense of the word "ministry" by liberating it from its bondage to service within the confines of the church. Ministry is service, and all those who have been called into a relationship with Christ are called to serve God and others in their various occupations.

Although this was a radical departure from the culture, it was not Luther's own invention. Indeed, the groundwork for recognizing the sacred value of ordinary life had already been laid both in Scripture and some of the church's own practices. It was implicit in the way the Old Testament regulated so many aspects of Israel's daily life. It was explicit in many New Testament directives that taught the church to do everything "for the glory of God" (1 Cor. 10:31; Col. 3:17, 23). Eating, drinking, family life, work, and even sex all fall under this rubric and are shown to be contexts in which the Christian can glorify God. The sacred nature of ordinary tasks was even embedded in the practice of monastic life. In *The Rule of Saint Benedict*, work was prescribed as one of means by which the monk served God. "In the Benedictine tradition, our labor is one way we participate in God's creative work of ordering Creation and bringing forth good fruit from it," Rod Dreher explains in his book *The Benedict Option*. "When undertaken in the right spirit, our labor is also a means God uses to order us inwardly."[7]

Modern evangelicals seem to have drifted away from Martin Luther's emphasis. Many churches today have reintroduced the division between secular and sacred by defining *ministry* narrowly to mean "church work." In this case, it is not a call to forsake the world by entering a monastery or taking holy orders. It is more a matter of limiting the church's interest and effort to those activities that promote its own advancement. *Ministry* is what the church does. The term is usually reserved for the church's programs. In my experience, much of the church's preaching seems intended to enlist the aid and involvement of the congregation in those activities while the rest goes largely ignored. A Christian who wants to do something meaningful for God can work with the church's youth or go on a short-term mission trip. They can work in the church's nursery or serve on a church committee. But the rest of what they do—which involves most of their life and activity—is pretty much a spiritual dead zone. It has relatively little value as far as the church is concerned. Oh sure, a certain level of moral behavior is expected and of course the church's members are expected to contribute some of what they earn to support the church's "ministries." But what church members are doing themselves is not treated as ministry. Serving our families, working at our jobs, and living in the community all fall outside the scope of meaningful service to God. No wonder they seem so unfulfilling to us.

There are hopeful signs that this mindset is changing. The modern-day faith-and-work or theology-of-work movement emphasizes the sanctity of ordinary work. However, Greg Forster, director of the Oikonomia Network at the Center for Transformational Churches at Trinity International University, notes that there is still more to be done. Forster explains that up until now, the movement has primarily focused on white-collar workers: "It doesn't speak very much to people who don't think of themselves as in the 'marketplace' traditionally understood, so teachers for example and stay-at-home moms, are not well-served in most cases by existing forms of the faith and work movement because the faith and work movement talks about the marketplace and many of them don't think of themselves as part of a marketplace."[8]

It is especially important for the church to reclaim Luther's vision of the sacred importance of those areas that have become secular in our thinking as a result of the church's neglect. Many of these areas are swiftly becoming cultural battle zones. But even more important, because the church fails to recognize the sacred value of ordinary life and defines ministry so narrowly, it does not equip its members to live Christianly in these areas. It may tell us how to order our own family or behave sexually, but it does not provide the training or support that will help us to bear witness in a culture that radically disagrees with the Bible's view on these matters. It does not even tell us how to do our jobs to the glory of God or be a neighbor in the community. Indeed, the impression that many churches give is that it is not especially interested in our ordinary lives at all. Only in our bodily presence, its portion of our paychecks, and whatever effort we can contribute to the success of its programs.

If ordinary life is sacred for the church's members, it is also sacred for its ministers and leaders. This means that church work is not the only meaningful thing that pastors and church leaders do. They care for their families and live in the community just like everyone else. They have hobbies. They read fiction and watch television. It also means that their ministry is also their job. We should not be surprised to find that it brings with it the drudgery and frustration that is common to all who work. Church leaders may labor in the Lord's vineyard, but their work is often painful toil just like everyone else's. Like the rest of humanity, they too must earn their living by the sweat of their brow (Gen. 3:17–19). To say that ordinary life is sacred does not mean that it is necessarily exciting or even pleasant. It simply means that ordinary life has value in God's sight. It is the context in which He does His work.

Practicing the Presence

Practicing the present will require us to reclaim a sense of the eternal significance of these mundane spaces in our lives. We don't do this by trying to change the quality of our experience in those areas. The mundane will still involve the mundane but by accepting the ordinary as a context in which God is present. The ordinary tasks assigned to us by our calling and life situation are no less meaningful to God than those that are extraordinary. We do not need to be attempting great things all the time. We do not need to make a name for ourselves. As far as we know from Scripture, Jesus spent most of the first thirty years of His earthly life doing very little that was worth writing about. He lived in Nazareth and worked an ordinary job. To the people in His hometown there didn't seem to be anything particularly special about Jesus. He was "the carpenter," just somebody from the village (Mark 6:3).

Those who practice the present give careful attention to the reality of God's presence in the world. They "practice the presence" of God. This was the subject of a series of letters written by Nicholas Herman, a lay brother in the Carmelite order who lived in France during the seventeenth century. Herman, who took the name Brother Lawrence, did not lead a sheltered life. He was born a peasant and was later a soldier and a servant. It was while contemplating a tree stripped of its leaves in the winter that Brother Lawrence first came to understand his need for God's grace. He was only eighteen at the time.

During his time in the monastery, Brother Lawrence was assigned to the kitchen. It was there that he concluded that his experience of God's presence as he carried out the mundane tasks of cooking and cleaning should be no different from his experience of God in prayer. Although we often view practicing the presence of God as a discipline, for Brother Lawrence it began with the realization that God is as close in the common business of ordinary life as He is in the sanctuary: "We need only to realize that God is close to us and to turn to Him at every moment, to ask for His help to do gladly those things which we clearly perceive He requires of us, offering to Him before we begin, and giving Him thanks when they have been finished for His honor."[9]

We do not need to resort to extraordinary acts of devotion to experience the reality of God's presence. Nor does the reality of God's nearness evaporate when we grow busy or our circumstances become difficult. During those times when we find it difficult to sense the nearness of God, He is as present as ever. From the highest heavens to the lowest depths, whatever situation we may find ourselves in is one in which God is already there (Ps. 139:8).

Although we always inhabit the present, we often feel as if it is moving past us. Try as we might to seize upon the moment and hold it fast, it still slips from our grasp. That good feeling we have passes or the season changes. The song that moved us so deeply comes to an end and somehow replaying it over again does not quite have the same effect. It is easy to think that we are standing fast as time marches past us and fades in the distance. We are caught in time's irresistible current and swept into the future. As much as we might want to revisit the past, we can do so only in our minds. We have moved beyond the past and cannot return to it, no matter what the science-fiction writers say. The future is as removed from us as the past. We may be moving inexorably toward it, but the future will always remain in front of us. We can only imagine or speculate what will take place there.

But God is the master of time. It serves God's purpose. The same God who established the regular cycle of day and night, summer and winter, seedtime and harvest, also orders the seasons of our lives (Gen. 8:22). Our times are in His hand (Ps. 31:15). God always acts on our behalf at the "right time" (Rom. 5:6). This was true of the birth of Jesus Christ, which occurred "when the set time had fully come" (Gal. 4:4). It is just as true in the commonplace things that concern us every day. Why do we brood about the past and fret over the future? According to Jesus, it is because we have lost sight of God. God gives meaning to the present. His presence sanctifies our boredom and redeems our discomfort. The present is more than a place where the past comes to rest. It is more than a staging ground for the future. The present is where God shows up.

Chapter 3

Race among the Ruins

Jesus says that each day has enough trouble of its own. This doesn't come as a surprise to us. We have had enough life experience to know that this is true. In a poem entitled *Preparedness*, Edwin Markham advises,

> *For all your days prepare,*
> *And meet them ever alike:*
> *When you are the anvil, bear—*
> *When you are the hammer, strike.*

Yet most of the time it seems as if we are neither the anvil nor the hammer but are caught between the two. Held in place against the anvil of circumstances that we cannot change, we are bent by the hammer of God's will. It is one thing to talk of practicing the present when life is ordinary. We can face the bread-and-butter struggles of daily living with some serenity, confident of God's presence. As long as we know that our problems are merely day visitors who show up for a few hours and then go on their way, we can easily put up with them. We might even be willing to bear with them for a few days or a few weeks because we know that in time, things will go back to normal. Our trials are unwelcome guests, but we say to ourselves, "This too shall pass before long."

But sometimes the circumstances that visit us arrive for the long term with no sign of leaving. They do not come for a short stay; they move in and become part of the family. My employer tells me that my position has been eliminated and that there is no other opportunity for me with the company. The doctor's diagnosis indicates that my condition will be prolonged without any certainty of treatment. My spouse decides to leave me, or my child says that he or she is gay. We have entered into a new "normal" in which boredom is the least of our problems. "Life changes in the instant. The ordinary instant," writer Joan Didion observed.[1] Suddenly, we hate our life as it currently is. The thought of practicing the present under such conditions not only appears foolish but seems cruel. How do we practice the present when the present is no longer a good place to be? It is almost impossible to offer an answer to such a question that does not sound glib.

Furthermore, the answer that we might offer while contemplating such circumstances from a distance is liable to be very different from the one we would give while suffering through them. The psalmist might well say, "It was good for me to be afflicted" (Ps. 119:71). But that is the perspective of someone after the trial is over. His tone is very different when he is in the midst of it. Then he cries, "How long, Lord? Will you forget me forever? How long will you hide your face from me? How long must I wrestle with my thoughts and day after day have sorrow in my heart? How long will my enemy triumph over me?" (Ps. 13:1–2).

The church has always tended to mistake stoicism for grace. That is why many of us are so inclined to offer platitudes in the face of suffering:

"Suck it up and tough it out."
"Look on the bright side."
"Things could be worse."

These are not the things we actually say, but the things we do say often amount to the same sentiment. We dress our platitudes for church, of course. We mention God and talk about things working together. We remind people of the blessings that will come out of this suffering and of the wisdom they will gain as a result. We tell them that obstacles are only opportunities in disguise. What we say is sometimes true and may even help. But they can't remove us from the circumstance. Our friends move on and return to their ordinary lives while we are left to contemplate what has happened to us. "Part of every misery is, so to speak, the misery's shadow or reflection: the fact that you don't merely suffer but have to keep on thinking about the fact that you suffer," C. S. Lewis observed. "I not only live each endless day in grief, but live each day thinking about living each day in grief."[2]

Are we really supposed to dwell on our own suffering?

Is that what it means to practice the present? Why wouldn't we want to be in some other situation? Like the psalmist, we want to say, "'Oh, that I had the wings of a dove! I would fly away and be at rest. I would flee far away and stay in the desert; I would hurry to my place of shelter, far from the tempest and storm'" (Ps. 55:6–8). Who wouldn't under such circumstances? It is important to understand that practicing the present does not necessarily mean that we want to remain in our present circumstances. It certainly does not mean that we enjoy the present, especially when that experience is marked by suffering. It also does not mean that we cease thinking about or planning for the future.

Those who practice the present are more than passive responders who merely allow themselves to be driven by their circumstances. The recognition that many of the things that affect us are beyond our control should not cause us to conclude that there is nothing we can do. This is especially important when it comes to suffering. "We must distinguish between those forms of suffering that happen to us and those we bring on ourselves," Stanley Hauerwas explains. "We not only suffer from diseases, accidents, tornadoes, earthquakes, droughts, and floods—all those things over which we have little control—but we also suffer from other people, from living here rather than there, from doing this kind of job—all matters we might avoid."[3]

Yet the fact that we are responsible agents whose actions have contributed to the situation in which we now find ourselves is often no comfort in the face of trouble. This knowledge might even put a sharper edge on our pain.

Not only must we cope with the consequences of our actions, we can't help considering what the alternative might have been if we had acted differently. If time is a stream, then the present is where the wreckage of the past comes to rest. Part of the work involved in practicing the present is sorting through this debris in an effort to understand how we may have contributed to our own circumstances. We may be engaging in a race among the ruins but it is often a ruin that we have partly made for ourselves. We are not the cause of all our problems but we are certainly the cause of some. Even those afflictions that trouble us, through no cause of our own, can be worsened by our response. This kind of reflection is difficult. Like Adam after his sin, we too are prone to denial and shifting blame. We are inclined to blame our neighbor and especially God for our problems.

Practicing the present in such times involves acknowledging our contribution and taking ownership of our actions. This can be uniquely difficult for pastors and other church leaders for multiple reasons. First, many of the actions we take as a church are a result of collective decision-making. Shifting blame is especially easy in such an environment. Like Aaron, leaders often find that they are more comfortable hiding behind the demands of the congregation rather than admitting that they share responsibility for the present circumstances (see Ex. 32:23–24). Second, leaders may be unwilling to admit their own foolish or sinful actions because they are afraid of the possible consequences of making such an admission. However, people usually admire a leader who admits their faults. Where sin is concerned, covering it is a bad strategy. Moses told the Israelites, "You may be sure that your sin will find you out" (Num. 32:23). The same could be said for leaders. Sooner or later, our sins will come to light. As for our mistakes, people usually recognize them long before we admit them.

Taking ownership of our actions is the first step in repentance. Likewise, taking ownership of the present is also an important step in coping with the discomfort that our problems cause, even when they are not the result of our own actions. "We often find that essential in our response to suffering is the ability to make what happens to me mine. Cancer patients frequently testify to some sense of relief when they find out they have cancer," Hauerwas explains. "The very ability to name what they have seems to give them a sense of control or possession that replaces the undifferentiated fear they had been feeling."[4]

It is not necessary to like our circumstances in order to own them in the way that Hauerwas describes. Nor does it necessarily result in a sense of complacency about the situation. Hauerwas points out that owning the suffering does not imply that every form of pain or suffering is good. "Extreme suffering can as easily destroy as enhance," he points out. "Nor do I suggest that we should be the kind of people can transform any suffering into benefit. We rightly feel that some forms of suffering can only be acknowledged, not transformed."[5] Those who take ownership of the present engage in a kind of mapping. They attempt to formulate an honest assessment of the situational, moral, and spiritual landscape.

As a pastor, I found that the hardest part of visiting church members at the hospital was leaving them in the same condition I found them when I entered the room. I felt that my visits should make a difference. If they did not, what good were they? On each occasion, I read Scripture, spoke words of comfort, and prayed. Yet when I was done, people often seemed no better off. It took me a long time to realize that my role was not to fix their problems but to exercise a ministry of presence. Every visit was a symbol of God's presence with them in the midst of their suffering. Scripture promised His control and care in even the worst circumstances. Prayer opened the door for God's involvement and served as a reminder that their suffering did not go unseen. Years after those visits, which seemed so impotent to me at the time, church members told me how much comfort they derived from them. This ministry of presence is an important pastoral tool in helping people take ownership of difficult circumstances that are beyond their control. It is a tangible reminder of Christ's own presence and His dominion over sickness, death, and destruction. "*The kingdom of God is where Jesus Christ is*," Helmut Thielicke observed. "But Jesus Christ always lingers in the darkest places in the world."[6]

Do Not Go Gentle

Practicing the present in the face of suffering should not be confused with despair. It involves a faith-based acceptance of things as they are. Perhaps a more accurate word for this is *surrender*. David demonstrated this kind of surrender as he faced two of the greatest tragedies in his life. Both circumstances involved his family and each was due in a large measure to his own sin. The first incident was the death of his and Bathsheba's son. Nathan had warned the king in advance that the child would die. "The LORD has taken away your sin. You are not going to die" the prophet told David after he repented. "But because by doing this you have shown utter contempt for the LORD, the son born to you will die" (2 Sam. 12:13–14). The prophet went home and the child got sick. David pleaded with God to spare the child's life. In what looks like an act of penance, David refused to eat and instead of sleeping in his bed at night, lay on the ground in sackcloth. Any parent who has sat by the bedside of a sick child can imagine how he must have felt. Yet for David, there was the added burden of knowing that it was his fault. Perhaps that was what gave David hope that his prayers might turn things around. The Lord struck the child. He could just as easily heal him.

But after seven days of illness, the child died. David's servants were unwilling to break the news to him fearing that he would do something desperate. When David noticed them whispering amongst themselves he guessed what had happened. "Is the child dead?" he asked. "Dead," they replied. Yet instead of going into mourning as expected, David got up and put on his regular clothes. He went to the house of the Lord and worshiped and then had something to eat. David's attendants were mystified. "Why are you acting this way?" they asked him. "While the child was alive, you fasted and wept, but now that the child is dead, you get up and eat!" David shrugged off the rebuke implied in the question. "While the child was still alive, I fasted and wept," he said. "I thought, 'Who knows? The LORD may be gracious to me and let the child live.' But now that he is dead, why should I go on fasting? Can I bring him back again? I will go to him, but he will not return to me."

David's prayers for the child were rooted in his hope that God might respond to his request with grace despite the fact that he was suffering from the consequences of his own actions. His acceptance of God's denial was grounded in a different hope. "I will go to him, but he will not return to me," David said. David was realistic in his assessment. But this was no despairing admission about the inevitability of death. His words were an affirmation of faith. They were grounded in David's hope of eternal life and his conviction that God was still working out His good plan even in this tragedy.

David's ability to face his radically changed present with hope was due in a large part to a conviction about the future. If it is true that the present is where the wreckage of the past comes to rest, it is equally true that God uses that wreckage to lay the foundation for the future. Either way, the work that needs to be done is in the present. Whether it is a matter of understanding the implications of the mistakes we have made in the past or learning how those mistakes have paved the way for the future, we must surrender to the life that God has for us in the present. We do this with the knowledge that God's hand is in our lives. He is at work even when the worst happens to us. David's experience is also a reminder that practicing the present by responding to our circumstances with faith-based surrender can sometimes be misunderstood by those around us. It may be interpreted as detachment, denial, and even callousness. Like David, we can explain the reasons for our hope but we cannot make others see what we see. In some cases, it will be impossible for them to understand unless they have shared a similar experience.

One of the most important tasks of pastoral care is that of helping people move on in hope when they have suffered a life-shattering event. Sometimes church leaders do this on an individual basis by patiently reminding their parishioners that it is okay to move on with normal life. Those who begin to do so are often racked with guilt. Going about our business after great loss seems callous, but it is really a way of healing. Moving on is an act of faith.

Puritan writer Jeremiah Burroughs described this as doing the work of our circumstances. "You should labor to bring your heart to quiet and contentment by setting your soul to work in the duties of your present condition," Burroughs explains. "And the truth is, I know nothing more effective for quieting a Christian soul and getting contentment than this, setting your heart to work in the duties of the immediate circumstances that you are now in, and taking heed of your thoughts about other conditions as a mere temptation."[7]

But let's be honest. Burroughs feels a little cold in his assessment. David likewise seems too businesslike. His recovery is too fast. Put on your clothes. Go have lunch. Comfort your wife. Move on. Is it really that simple?

The answer is no. The Bible's account of David's experience is vivid but spare. The author is making a point by not giving us a psychological analysis. We do not have the advantage of seeing David's reactions close up. We do not hear the conversation he had with Bathsheba when he went to her to offer comfort. We do not see the remainder of their tears or hear them as they weep together after the fact. Did they talk about their regrets? It would be a mistake to assume that David's grief magically disappeared when he surrendered to the situation. But David did move on. He did, to use the language of Jeremiah Burroughs, attend to the duties of the immediate circumstances.

Church leaders are also sometimes called to help people move on collectively after a congregational trauma. It may be a church split or a failure of leadership. In such cases, moving on usually begins with an acknowledgement of what has taken place. To continue on as if nothing has happened is simply a form of denial. Healing begins when the church's leaders help the congregation take stock of what has happened. In the beginning, this is simply a matter of recounting what took place. In time, however, recounting should lead to accounting. Is confession of sin or admission of error required in order for the church to move on? Does forgiveness need to be asked for or granted? In cases where the church's leaders have been complicit, they must own up to their fault and begin the work of rebuilding. This is an act of faith on two important levels. Leaders who own up to their bad decisions and failures are exercising faith in the congregation. They are also exercising faith in God. By their actions, leaders who do this show that they expect God's people to respond with patience and grace. This will happen only if those leaders have modeled patience and grace in their own ministry. They also show that they expect God to continue to work out His good purpose for the church despite their errors.

One instance where we see David respond to tragedy with this kind of faith-based acceptance of his circumstances was also occasioned by a family crisis. It happened when David's son Absalom went off the rails. Like the death of David's son by Bathsheba, this tragedy was rooted in David's own failure. According to 2 Samuel 12:11–12, Nathan predicted not only the death of Bathsheba's son, but also the collapse of David's family. The prediction was fulfilled when Absalom mounted an attempted coup and David was forced to flee across the Kidron Valley into the desert (2 Sam. 15:13–37). David left the city with his head covered in shame, weeping as he went (v. 30).

As the procession moved out of the city, Abiathar and Zadok brought the ark of the covenant, intending to carry it into exile with the king. But David told them to take the ark of God back into the city, saying, "If I find favor in the LORD's eyes, he will bring me back and let me see it and his dwelling place again. But if he says, 'I am not pleased with you,' then I am ready; let him do to me whatever seems good to him" (2 Sam. 15:25–26).

Is this faith or fatalism? It does not seem like fatalism,

if only because David took practical steps to protect his interests. He directed Zadok and Abiathar to return to the city and act as his eyes and ears (v. 28). He also told Hushai to return and feign allegiance to Absalom in the hope that he would be able to frustrate the counsel of Ahithophel, a trusted adviser to David who had defected to the other side (v. 34). This measure saved David's life (2 Sam. 17:1–16). But David's view of his circumstances went beyond the practical. He had a theological view as well. He recognized that his future was in God's hands. God will do "whatever seems good to him."

When we surrender to our circumstances, we continue to act responsibly within those circumstances. Yet we are inevitably affected by them. Indeed, one of the chief tasks we face when we accept painful circumstances is the challenge of working through the difficulties that come with those circumstances. Faith does not magically make our grief or anxiety disappear. We are not transported emotionally into some other realm so we do not have to deal with the emotional trauma of what has happened to us. Eventually, our appetite returns. We put on our clothes and go back to work. We pick up the kids from school and feed the dog. But it's not as if nothing has changed. Everything has changed.

The same holds true for church leaders. One of the greatest difficulties of living through personal or congregational trauma is the fact that the new normal does not relieve us of the responsibilities of the old life. Pastors must still write sermons week after week. The sick need to be visited. Committees still need direction. Ordinary decisions must be made. Although tending to the mundane tasks of ministry may initially feel like a great chore, God uses these ordinary responsibilities to help us adapt to a changed environment. Their familiarity, as dull as it may seem when compared to the adrenaline rush of crisis, is a comforting reminder that there really is something normal about the new normal. Even when circumstances change radically, our lives and ministries go on.

Practicing the present does not deliver us from turmoil. The practice does not transfer us into a special state of grace that somehow enables us to float above our circumstances so that we feel untouched by them. We may experience regret. We can be confused about what we should do next. We might feel afraid. We may even be angry enough to scream and sad enough to weep. Or we may feel nothing at all as we seek a temporary respite from our circumstances in the numbness of shock. Yet this raises obvious questions: If practicing the present is unable to deliver us from the frailty that attends all mortals when they find themselves in great difficulty, what good is it? What exactly does it do for us?

The answer is that it delivers us into the hands of God. Jesus' reminder that every day has enough trouble of its own is not a warning. It is a road sign. Jesus points us in the direction of God's presence. His statement is actually the concluding observation in a series of observations about the kingdom in Matthew 6:25–34. It follows on the heels of His culminating command to seek the kingdom above everything else. This may seem like comparing apples and oranges. What does the kingdom have to do with my troubles? By connecting the troubles of the day with the command to seek first the kingdom, isn't Jesus really teaching us to do the opposite of practicing the present? Focus on the future instead. "Your life may be full of problems today," He seems to say, "but cheer up because there's a better world coming."

Jesus is clearly saying something about the future here. The future is real. It is what the present is moving toward. He is also implying something about the kingdom. If we are seeking the kingdom, it cannot have arrived yet—at least not in its full measure. There is a kingdom to come, just as there is a future to come. This is how Jesus taught us to pray in Matthew 6:10: "Your kingdom come, your will be done, on earth as it is in heaven." There is both conflict and continuity implied in these words. On one hand, it is a request that implies that our present circumstance is not what we would like. On the other, it teaches us to expect the extension of the divine order, which already exists in heaven and on earth as well.

The earth upon which we now live is God's domain. Psalm 24:1–2 declares, "The earth is the LORD's, and everything in it, the world, and all who live in it; for he founded it on the seas and established it on the waters." The earth belongs to the Lord by right because He is its Creator. Yet for now, the earth is also a domain in rebellion. Satan's presence has turned it into a battle zone of conflicting dominions. Satan is "the spirit who is now at work in those who are disobedient" (Eph. 2:2). The collateral damage produced by this insurrection is social as well as spiritual. In his effort to take God's place, Satan has introduced a competing set of values and practices that are opposed to God's. The consequences of Satan's rebellion against God are also physical. When Adam sinned, creation itself was subjected to decay (Rom. 8:21). So, even creation itself has been drawn into this struggle. The universe is a place of terror as well as beauty. As far as we can tell, the majority of it is uninhabitable by humans. Even in our habitable corner of it, we often face hazards that threaten to destroy us.

We are not the only ones who long for this to change. "We know that the whole creation has been groaning as in the pains of childbirth right up to the present time," Paul observes. "Not only so, but we ourselves, who have the firstfruits of the Spirit, groan inwardly as we wait eagerly for our adoption to sonship, the redemption of our bodies" (Rom. 8:22–23). How is it possible to practice the present when creation itself seems to be leaning into the future? Here we come to another important corrective. Practicing the present does not mean that we are satisfied with the present. We can practice the present and long for the future at the same time. Practicing the present is not some Jedi mind trick intended to convince us that everything is wonderful when, in fact, things are terrible. It is not an exercise of mind over matter that we employ to make our emotional or physical pain disappear. Those who practice the present effectively recognize that they are living in occupied territory. But they also understand that when the Father raised

Jesus from the dead, He "seated him at his right hand in the heavenly realms, far above all rule and authority, power and dominion, and every name that is invoked, not only in the present age but also in the one to come" (Eph. 1:20–21). Satan, as the "god of this age," exercises a kind of rule over the earth. Yet Jesus exercises a greater dominion. Jesus' dominion does more than surpass Satan's authority. Christ's dominion transcends it. Jesus is not merely above Satan; He is "far above" him, as well as above every other rule, authority, power, dominion, and name.

When we pray "Your kingdom come, your will be done, on earth as it is in heaven," we are praying for God to manifest His rule at the intersection of heaven and earth. It is a prayer that asks for the rule of heaven be manifest on earth. It will find its ultimate fulfillment in the future when Jesus Christ comes again to reign on earth. But make no mistake about it, this prayer is designed for the present. Like the other petitions of the Lord's Prayer that are focused on the here and now, this is a request for God to act in the present. We are indeed looking forward to a world governed by the rule of heaven; but for the present, we need intervention.

This particular petition of the Lord's Prayer implies two important facts about the relationship between heaven and earth. The first will come as no surprise. It is what your experience has already shown you. Heaven is not earth. There is a distinction between the two. But heaven is more than a state of mind; it actually exists, just as earth exists. Jesus came from heaven and returned to heaven (John 3:13). Heaven is where Christ now dwells in bodily form and is enthroned

(Col. 3:1). The second assumption is equally important: although heaven is distinct from earth, it exists in proximity to earth. New Testament scholar N. T. Wright explains that the relationship between the two is one of dimension: "Basically, heaven and earth in biblical cosmology are not two different locations within the same continuum of space or matter." Further, "They are two different dimensions of God's good creation."[8] Because they are dimensionally related though separate, they share a kind of proximity. According to Wright, this is implied in the bodily ascension of Christ into heaven. "What we are encouraged to grasp precisely through the ascension itself is that God's space and ours—heaven and earth, in other words—are, though very different, not far away from one another."[9]

The Lord's Prayer teaches us to expect the rule of heaven to intersect not only our world but our lives as well. It can do so at any moment and in any circumstance. It also has the power to redeem our most broken circumstances. Helmut Thielicke described the relationship with these striking words: "In, with, and under the world's anguish and distress, in, with, and under the hail of bombs and mass murders, God is building his kingdom."[10] Church leaders might say the same. In, with, and under our imperfect leadership, mistakes, and even our sins, God is accomplishing His good purposes for us and for our congregation.

This heavenly perspective sheds new light on the command of Colossians 3:1–2, which tells us to set our hearts on things above. Far from being a call to ignore the present along with its circumstances, these verses invite us to expand our vision of the present. We must see more than the difficulties that plague us. They are real enough. But heaven is also real. Indeed, as Paul describes it, heaven is more real because that is where our life is now hidden: "For you died, and your life is now hidden with Christ in God. When Christ, who is your life, appears, then you also will appear with him in glory" (Col. 3:3–4). Not only do heaven and earth intersect in this verse, but so do the present and the future. What will be true is already true. The life that is now hidden in Christ will one day be revealed when Christ appears. Our ultimate hope lies in the future. Yet the call to live is grounded firmly in the present.

In view of these truths, how do we practice the present when we feel that we have been caught between the anvil and the hammer? Some pastors feel trapped because they are serving a church that has not lived up to their expectations. They would like to relocate to a more responsive congregation, but none have expressed an interest in hiring them. Others have the opposite problem. They were forced out of a church they loved and hoped to continue to serve. Some church leaders are living with regret because of foolish or sinful choices that have ongoing consequences they cannot escape. Many more are simply trying to cope with the same kind of problems that everyone else faces: a wayward child, the death of a spouse, or an unwanted medical diagnosis.

How do we practice the present in these kinds of situations? We must first of all surrender in hope. Acknowledge the true nature of your circumstances along with all their unwelcome consequences. You do not need to put a good face on a bad situation. You do not need to put on a happy face. You do not need to pretend that you feel anything other than you do feel about it all. But you do need to accept the situation as it now is along with all your feelings about it. This may be particularly difficult for church leaders, who often feel pressured to keep up appearances. Pastors are supposed to have answers, not ask questions. They help others who are in doubt. They point the way of forgiveness to others but do not sin themselves. Of course, none of these assumptions are true. It is a great help to a congregation when it can see how its leaders work through the same kind of struggles they also face. The desire to keep up appearances is really just a form of pride. It is also a form of denial. Although it may make us feel better in the short term, it will eventually take its toll on us and on everyone around us.

Second, take stock of the situation. This involves the kind of assessment described earlier. How did we get here? What was beyond our control? What did we contribute to the situation? It is helpful to distinguish between circumstances we have created by our own choices and those that are beyond our control. This is an analysis of the present that takes the past into account. Sometimes, the mess we must deal with is one of our own making. Often, it is something we inherited.

As we take stock, we take responsibility. We are by nature prone to blame-shifting and denial like our forefather Adam. Leaders are especially adept at shifting the burden of responsibility either to the congregation or even to God Himself. Just as King Saul when he disobeyed

God at Gilgal, we justify our actions by blaming others or pointing to our circumstances (1 Sam. 13:10–14). When we practice the present, we seek by God's grace to resist this tendency and make a full accounting. Did we make choices in our personal lives or our ministry that we should not have? The fact that we regret a choice does not automatically mean that we have sinned, but where sin is involved, we must acknowledge it and confess.

The other important assessment that must be made is more practical. What do we need to do now? The answer to this question is usually very concrete. It is unromantic. Do the dishes. Set the alarm and get up for work in the morning. Read your Bible. Pray. Walk the dog. Balance the checkbook. Pay the bills. Engage in polite conversation with your neighbor. Most of the rhythms connected with practicing the present involve the ordinary activities of common life. Church leaders are often tempted to disparage these things when compared to the higher tasks of ministry. They are not mysterious, nor are they glamorous. They are not in themselves especially spiritual or even difficult, yet they often seem wearisome in times of crisis. We don't know where we will find the energy for them. One reason is that these ordinary disciplines are already small and tend to shrink even more when they are compared with our suffering. Our suffering is so great and these common tasks are so trivial. How can we even think of taking them up again?

It takes great courage to "do the work of our circumstances" by tending to the business at hand. Focusing on mundane tasks feels like an act of defiance. It can be physically demanding to engage in some of the most ordinary duties, especially when grief, anxiety, or illness have robbed us of our energy. But doing the work of our circumstances by tending to the ordinary is also an act of faith. By tending to the present, we are also saying that we are open to the future. Like David, we are moving on along the path that God has ordained for us. Great trials intrude on our ordinary lives in a way that shakes us out of our lethargy and compels us to move into spiritual territory we would otherwise avoid. Returning to the mundane not only helps us to reenter normal life but enables us to integrate the lessons we've learned.

The third thing we must do as we practice the present in times of grief, pain, or difficulty is keep an eye open for the intersection of heaven and earth. I do not mean by this that our difficult circumstances will suddenly be transformed into heaven on earth. Nor am I suggesting that if you practice the present, God will magically make all the bad things that have happened to you disappear. Things can always get worse. What I can promise you is that if you look for God in the midst of your circumstances, you will find Him. Our afflictions act as a goad whose uncomfortable prodding compels us to follow paths we would not have chosen otherwise. The landscape may appear barren. It may seem to you that you have been abandoned. Even though you may not sense Christ's presence in the midst of your circumstances, you can trace His proximity on the map of His promise: "I will never leave you or forsake you. I will be with you always, even to the very end of the age" (Matt. 28:20).

Chapter 4

Living on Daily Bread

My mother grew up in Regina, Saskatchewan, during the Great Depression. At one time, her father had money, with a diamond stickpin and a string of movie theaters. But the crash of 1929, his habit of gambling away his money, and alcohol robbed him of it all. The stories she told us of her childhood reminded me of *The Little Rascals*, but without the laughter. At one point, she even begged her mother to ask a wealthy family to adopt her. There were many days when she didn't know where she would find her next meal. She said that some weeks, all her entire family had to eat was a can of beans that they shared between the five of them. On many days, they had nothing to eat at all.

I didn't enjoy hearing my mother's stories. Often, after she had launched into one, I asked her to stop. I was disturbed by the thought that she had suffered such deprivation. I couldn't imagine what it would be like to wonder whether there would be enough food for the next meal. I worried that if such a thing could happen to her, the same thing might happen to me.

No wonder I was worried. Few things are more basic to life than daily bread. One of the first lessons God taught the fledgling nation of Israel was the importance of living on daily bread. During their sojourn in the wilderness, He provided daily bread for Israel in form of manna (Ex. 16:1–36). The lesson of manna was not about deprivation or even simplicity. It was about sustenance:

> Remember how the LORD your God led you all the way in the wilderness these forty years, to humble and test you in order to know what was in your heart, whether or not you would keep his commands. He humbled you, causing you to hunger and then feeding you with manna, which neither you nor your ancestors had known, to teach you that man does not live on bread alone but on every word that comes from the mouth of the LORD. (Deut. 8:2–3)

The qualifying word "alone" is significant. It is an acknowledgment of genuine need. We do not live by bread alone, but we do need bread. Indeed, the fact that God supplied Israel with bread on a daily basis shows just how real this need is. The Lord's provision came with an important stipulation: They were to gather only as much as was needed for the day (Ex. 16:19). They were not permitted to store up manna for the future. If they did, the manna would become full of maggots and smell. The one exception had to do with the Sabbath. On the sixth day, God's people were required to collect twice as much so they would have food on the Sabbath. No manna fell on the Sabbath day. On the

Sabbath, what had been collected the previous day did not spoil. The lesson is powerful. We live by God's power. He is the one who sustains us. It is true that we need to eat, but we do not live by food alone.

The Importance of Daily Bread

Jesus quoted the last part of Deuteronomy 8:3 when Satan challenged Him to turn the stones into bread in order to prove that He was truly the Son of God (Matt. 4:1–4). Jesus also taught His disciples to pray for "daily bread" in the Lord's Prayer (Matt. 6:11; Luke 11:3). There is a slight difference in the form in Luke's version, but the essence of the request is unchanged (Luke 11:2–4).

The language used in Jesus' prayer underscores a subtle but important point. Some of our most important needs are not long term. They are not like our investment portfolio, savings account, or even our ten-year plan for ministry. The need for food is both immediate and recurring. It is a need that, once it is met, returns every single day. Even if I ate yesterday, I will be hungry again today. Some of our most important needs are also time sensitive. The fact that the need was met yesterday does not tell me how it will be met today. Today's meal, once it has been consumed, will not fill me tomorrow.

Some scholars want to spiritualize this request by linking it with the messianic age. But taking the request in its ordinary sense does not detract from the spiritual implications it may have in the age to come. Jesus knew full well how important eating and drinking are to human existence. One of the criticisms of Jesus' enemies was that He "came eating and drinking" (Matt. 11:19). What we call the Last Supper was really the culmination of many meals that Jesus took with His followers. The Gospels describe Jesus eating ordinary meals with His disciples, both before and after His resurrection. This experience shaped the way the early church viewed its own eating. Historian Andrew McGowan notes, "These narratives reflect the early Christians' sense of their community meals as the continuation of a whole series of Jesus' suppers or banquets, not just a response to or memorialization of one."[1]

It is difficult for many of us to grasp the reality of our complete dependence on God for daily bread, as well as the sacred significance of our ordinary eating. For most of us, a day has never gone by when we have had to wonder where our next meal will come from or whether we would eat at all. If we are hungry, we need only open the refrigerator. If we don't like what we find there, we can go to a restaurant or stop at the store. We are consumers in both senses of the word. We consume what we eat but we are also accustomed to having what we eat marketed to us. Our prosperity affords us the luxury of being able to choose what we will eat and when we will eat it. The supply is vast, and the selection is often overwhelming. What kind of daily bread do you want? Whole wheat, white, or multigrain? Gluten-free or vegan? Food manufacturers spend billions of dollars trying to process, package, and display food that will appeal to us.

At the same time, this abundance, which is unmatched in the history of the world, has made slaves of us. Not only are we slaves to the particularity of our tastes, but we have become slaves to those who want to shape those tastes for us. Wendell Berry has pointed out that most eaters these days are passive consumers. "They buy what they want—or what they have been persuaded to want—within the limits of what they can get," he explains. "They pay, mostly without protest, what they are charged."[2] It seems as though we can get almost anything, but that does not necessarily mean that we can always get what we want. We can only get what is made available to us. It certainly does not mean that we can always get what we really need or what is good for us. Berry points out that specialization of production leads to specialization of consumption. To explain how this affects our eating, Berry points to the entertainment industry as an analogy: "Patrons of the entertainment industry, for example, entertain themselves less and less and have become more and more passively dependent on commercial suppliers."[3]

Anybody who has spent hours scanning the vast selection offered by their cable provider only to give up in disgust, or settle for something they have already watched once or twice before and for which they are paying too much, will understand his point. Just as we have lost the capacity to entertain ourselves and must now settle for options chosen for us by the entertainment industry, we have also lost the ability to eat for ourselves. We are dependent on food that has been selected and prepared for us by those who are far more interested in our wallet than our health, despite the nutritional information on the back of the package. We are what Berry calls industrial eaters. "The industrial eater is, in fact, one who does not know that eating is an agricultural act, who no longer knows or imagines the connections between eating and the land, and who is therefore necessarily passive and uncritical—in short, a victim."[4] Perhaps Berry's language is too strong. We certainly have some say in what we eat and stores are becoming increasingly aware that some of their customers are consumers with a conscience. But in the end, we are still treated like consumers.

Eating Is a Community Enterprise

Eating and the economy are obviously linked. We must buy our daily bread since most of us do not produce it for ourselves. Those who do produce food are in the business of selling it. But eating is a matter of economy in a much larger and more theological sense. The term *economy* comes from the Greek word for household. It speaks of more than buying or selling. An economy is really an ecosystem. It is part of a larger whole. In this respect, every community is also an economy. Daily bread is much more than an individual act of consumption; it is a community enterprise. The communal implications of eating are evidenced all through Scripture. They are embedded in the Law of Moses, which required growers to leave behind the grain that was dropped in order to provide for the poor (Lev. 19:9–10; see also Ruth 2). They are implied in the biblical rule of hospitality, an exercise that always involved eating (Rom. 12:13; 16:23; 1 Tim. 5:10; Heb. 13:2; 1 Peter 4:9).

The link between eating and communion was especially evident in the practice of sacrificial meals. Several of Israel's sacrifices involved eating in God's presence. This was most vividly portrayed in Exodus 24, which describes how the elders of Israel ate and drank in God's presence. In 1 Corinthians 10:18, Paul calls those who offered such sacrifices *participants* in the altar. In saying this, he seems to be drawing a parallel with the Lord's Supper in an effort to persuade the Corinthians to abstain from participation in pagan idol feasts (1 Cor. 10:16, 17, 21). Eating is a communal activity that is tied to the means of production and the well-being of the community at large, but it is also a sacred act. In other words, our problem is more than the fact that we have been turned into industrial eaters. Our chief difficulty is that we have become secular eaters. Many of us fail to see the connection between God and our daily bread. Food is still a common feature of the church's life, but eating is not viewed as a context in which we experience fellowship with God. Indeed, we do not even see our observation of the Lord's Supper as a meal in any real sense. Many of us regard it as a valuable symbol but do not consider it to be spiritually sustaining in any meaningful way.

An economy is also a way of organizing and administrating. In theology, we sometimes speak of God's economy when referring to His divine plan for humanity. By God's design, reliance on daily bread is the central element of our most fundamental economy. We must eat in order to live, and if we are to eat, we must procure food. This is a daily task that involves a complex interdependency not only of ourselves with others but of ourselves with creation itself. This connection was established at creation when Adam was placed in the garden to "work it and take care of it" (Gen. 2:15).

This language is significant, especially since it describes Adam's vocation prior to creation's fall. Despite our mental image of Eden as a place where fruit was simply there for the picking, it is clear that even before the fall, Adam's quest for daily bread involved a measure of effort. The garden was filled with food. Adam was free to eat from all of the trees except one (Gen. 2:16). However, the language of verse 15 implies that even those trees whose fruit was permitted required tending. The Hebrew word that is translated as "work" in verse 15 also means "to serve." By virtue of creation, Adam was a child of God. By virtue of his calling, he was a servant of the garden. He was placed in the garden for that purpose. This vocation was a community effort, one that Adam shared with Eve (Gen. 2:18). The nature of their calling is further described in verse 15 as being one of stewardship. Adam was placed in the garden to serve and to "take care of it." This Hebrew verb expresses the idea of watchfulness or protection. The garden sustained humanity with its fruit and in some measure was itself sustained by those who inhabited it.

In addition, the garden was a context in which Adam and Eve experienced the presence of God. Genesis 3:8 uses relational imagery when it speaks of God "walking in the garden in the cool of the day." Although Adam and Eve hid as soon as they became aware of His presence, the scene itself intimates that this was not always the case. Adam and Eve's attempt to hide from God in Genesis 3:8 is merely the first tremor of a much greater disruption that is described in the rest of the Bible's pages. Adam's sin and its aftershocks have not only separated us from God but from the sacred connection between our need for daily bread and the vocation we employ in order to obtain it. "More and more, we take for granted that work must be destitute of pleasure. More and more, we assume that if we want to be pleased, we must wait until evening, or the weekend, or vacation, or retirement," Wendell Berry explains. "More and more, our farms and forests resemble our factories and offices, which in turn more and more resemble prisons—why else should we be so eager to escape them?"[5]

God has sent the church into this fallen world and charged its leaders with the task of making disciples (Matt. 28:18–20). One aspect of this task is to help the church recapture God's vision for the world He has made. Their goal is not to take God's people back to Eden or even to turn the fallen world into a garden. It is to help them live in this post-fall world as God intended.

Finding Daily Bread in a Fallen World

Sin has degraded our vocation into drudge work, our feasts to bare consumption, and our community to a collection of individuals who vie for their own interests. Sin did not drive God's presence from the world, but it does make us prone to suppress our awareness of its reality (Rom. 1:18). In the Genesis account, we find that four of the most fundamental aspects of human life are interrelated: the need for daily bread, work, community life, and fellowship with God. But in the post-fall world, the connection between those spheres has been broken.

It is here that Jesus chooses to engage with us on this subject. He does not speak about our quest for daily bread from the comfort of Eden before the fall. He faces it head-on in the broken world through which we now must make our way. His message to us is that the God who provided for our needs in the garden continues to provide for us in the fallen world. He teaches us to pray that our heavenly Father will provide our daily bread (Matt. 6:11; Luke 11:3). He tells us not to be anxious about what we will eat, drink, or wear because our heavenly Father knows we need these things (Matt. 6:31–32).

But how can we not be anxious in a world where the ground that bears its fruit also produces thorns and thistles and where we must eat our bread by the sweat of our brow? Jesus' commands seem counterintuitive. This is because we have believed two lies. One is that we are primarily responsible for what we have. We believe it is up to us to provide for ourselves. We are anxious about these things because we feel that the burden of obtaining daily bread primarily rests on our shoulders. Church leaders often transfer this false work ethic into the realm of ministry. They are convinced that the success of their ministry is up to them. As a result, leaders often feel responsible for burdens that should be shouldered by God, or they take credit for results that do not belong to them.

When I first became a follower of Jesus, I decided a good way to signal the change to my family was to begin praying before meals. The first time I did this, my father became angry. "Why are you thanking God for the food?" he demanded. "You should thank *me*. My money paid for it. I cooked it." There was some truth in what he said. Daily bread does not suddenly appear on our plates when mealtime arrives. Even if it did, we would still need to make an effort to eat it. There is a connection between our effort and God's provision. In 2 Thessalonians 3:10, Paul the tradesman links eating with working: "For even when we were with you, we gave you this rule: 'The one who is unwilling to work shall not eat.'"

Certainly there are some who are unable to work. The church has an obligation to assist those who cannot provide for themselves. One of the core community values of the New Testament church was to share with any in the community of believers who had need (Acts 2:45; 4:35). But under ordinary circumstances, the link between work and our daily bread that was established in Eden still holds. Most of the time, our bread does not fall from heaven. We must work if we are to eat. Yet we should not let the fact that we can and do work deceive us into thinking that we are providing for ourselves without God.

God often provides for us through ordinary means. It is foolish to miss seeing His hand in the process simply because it is extended to us by means of a secondary agency, even if we are the agent. Both our capacity to work and the opportunity to do so come from Him. Whether we buy the bread from the store or bake it ourselves from scratch, it still ultimately comes from God.

Yet it is equally a mistake to confuse the means that God uses to provide for us with God Himself. When we do this, we become like the idol worshiper described in Isaiah 44 who fashions an idol from a tree: "Half of the wood he burns in the fire; over it he prepares his meal, he roasts his meat and eats his fill. He also warms himself and says, 'Ah! I am warm; I see the fire.' From the rest he makes a god, his idol; he bows down to it and worships. He prays to it and says, 'Save me! You are my god!'" (Isa. 44:16–17). This error mistakes the gift for the giver and expects more from what has been given than it can possibly provide.

This was Jesus' point when Satan tempted Him to turn stones into bread. We need daily bread, but bread is not the ultimate source of our life. God alone sustains us, no matter what means He may use. Jesus illustrated this truth in the parable of the rich fool in Luke 12:16–21. The rich man's ground produced a crop so large that his barns could not contain it. The man resolved to tear down his barns and build bigger ones. In Jesus' parable, God calls the man a fool. Yet why would God take issue with his plan? It seems like common sense to us. We would probably do the same if we were in his shoes. Despite all his planning, the man's problem was ultimately one of limited vision. He had planned only for the long term. He expected to take life easy because he had "plenty of grain laid up for many years"

(v. 19). Unfortunately, he forgot to take the short term into account. "You fool! This very night your life will be demanded from you," God says in the parable. "Then who will get what you have prepared for yourself?" (v. 20).

Our Lives Are Not Our Own

Such language is a sharp reminder that our lives are not really our own. They belong to God. In His explanation of the parable, Jesus condemned the rich man's long range plan too. Not for its pragmatism, but because of the atheistic nature of the assumption that guided it. The man in the story is an example of one who trusts in the things that God has provided but is not "rich toward God" (v. 21). This was Jesus' starting point. He told the parable when someone in the crowd demanded that Jesus tell his brother to divide the family inheritance with him (Luke 12:13). Jesus' reply seems unfeeling to us. Jesus answered, "Man, who appointed me a judge or an arbiter between you?" Who should we turn to in such matters if not to Jesus? We would tend to see this request as a question of justice. But Jesus saw through the man's question and discovered a different motive. "Watch out!" Jesus told the crowd who had heard His parable. "Be on your guard against all kinds of greed; life does not consist in an abundance of possessions" (Luke 12:15).

Greed takes a variety of forms. We tend to think of it as the besetting sin of the rich. Since many of us presume we are not rich, we conclude that we are not greedy. We may be putting ourselves in spiritual danger by thinking this way, positioning ourselves in a way that guarantees that Jesus' warning will miss the mark. Greed has to do with wanting as much as it does with having. It is just as easy for a poor man to be greedy as a rich one. Indeed, it may even be easier, since there is so much more to want. Every age and culture has had to struggle with greed. It is notable that two of the seven sins that the church has traditionally identified as capital sins fall under this heading: gluttony and avarice.

Gluttony is generally associated with food. But that is probably too narrow. Gluttony isn't just about what we put in our stomach; it is about what we desire. Gluttony is the sin of an inordinate appetite. Although it has been traditionally seen as a sin of eating too much, it is more accurate to say that gluttony is the sin of seeking ultimate satisfaction from the wrong source. Avarice is a related sin that is most often associated with money but can be directed toward just about anything. Avarice can be expressed as the quest for more money, power, fame, or pretty much whatever you can desire. If gluttony is the sin of inordinate desire, then avarice may be a sin of inordinate possession. There seems to be an implication in Jesus' parable that the rich fool wanted to hold on to more than was good for him. He did not consider the possibility that God might have meant the abundance that had been put in his hands to go to someone else. Indeed, he did not consider God at all, which was at the heart of his failure.

Most of us, if we are honest, do not identify with the rich fool. We build modest garages, not bigger barns. We are not worried about finding enough room to store all our stuff. We are trying to pay off the few things we have. Nevertheless, we have been trained to share the rich fool's values from our earliest age. Philosopher James K. A. Smith warns that we have been discipled into a catechism of greed by being immersed in something he calls "mall religion." Smith claims that the shopping mall is a religious institution because it is both liturgical and formative. It is liturgical in the sense that it involves practices that are both repeated and familiar. It is formative because it subtly instills within us a view of the world and a set of values. The context is so familiar that our behavior when we visit it is a reflex, a kind of whole-life muscle memory. But each time we engage in these practices, a vision of what is important is imprinted upon us. Smith uses the mall as an example to show how many secular liturgies affect us. These ordinary practices shape our responses and embed values: "In short, they are meaning laden, identity-forming practices that subtly shape us precisely because they grab hold of our love—they are automating our desire and action without our conscious recognition."[6]

Why did Jesus tell the parable of the rich fool? Was it because He doesn't want us to have nice things? Maybe it's that He doesn't want us to have *many* things, so that we will learn to be content with just a few. It turns out that it's not the things at all that are the problem. It is the way we have been viewing ourselves in relation to them. Jesus revealed His point before He told the parable: "Watch out! Be on your guard against all kinds of greed; life does not consist in an abundance of possessions."

Why should we be on guard against greed? Because greed will not sustain us in the end. Greed cannot sustain us because it comes from a hunger that will never be satiated and a thirst that can never be slaked. No matter how many of our desires are met, our appetite always seems to expand. No matter how full our barns may be, we would always like to have a little more. But the real weakness of greed is that it misses the mark entirely. Our life originates somewhere else. It comes from God and is sustained by Him. He is not jealous of our things. He does not need them. "The God who made the world and everything in it is the Lord of heaven and earth and does not live in temples built by human hands," the apostle Paul told the philosophers on Mars Hill. "And he is not served by human hands, as if he needed anything. Rather, he himself gives everyone life and breath and everything else" (Acts 17:24–25).

Jesus does not say that our daily bread will come without effort, but rather that we must not think about these things like orphans. "Thank God that this Father is so compassionate and realistic that he appraises the little things in our life (included a warm sweater and our daily bread) at exactly the same value that they actually have in our life," Helmut Thielicke observes. "Thank God that he accepts us just as we are, as living men, with great dreams, but also with many little desires and fears, with hunger and weariness and the thousand and one pettinesses and pinpricks of life that fill even the lives of the great of this earth (one need only to read their memoirs)."[7]

How Then Shall We Eat?

Wendell Berry writes that many times, after he has lectured on the decline of American farming and rural life, people ask him, "What can city people do?" His reply? "Eat responsibly."[8] That's pretty good advice for everyone. Responsible eating includes more than social awareness. It involves spiritual awareness as well. Our life does not consist in an abundance of things (Luke 12:15). It does not even consist in our daily bread. Even though food is necessary for our survival, our life is found in God. The ordinary practice of partaking of daily bread is the chief sacrament of that life. God sets the table by providing daily bread and acts as our host. Every ordinary meal points to the inevitability of God's care. Each bite we take is a reminder of Christ's promise that the Father knows what we need.

Every ordinary meal is a feast too—not so much because of the menu, which may only be made up of simple fare, but because of the rich company that we enjoy as we partake. Most of our meals are eaten in the company of family or friends whom we love. Even if we eat alone, we are still in the company of God, who is always and everywhere present with us. He is there in our most difficult circumstances when our appetite deserts us. He will be there even should our family and friends forsake us. He prepares a table for us in the presence of our enemies, treats us as a special guest, and fills our cup until it overflows (Ps. 23:5).

RULES FOR EATING RESPONSIBLY

The Bible offers some guidelines for responsible eating. Not surprisingly, they have as much to do with the soul as they do with the body:

- The first principle of responsible eating is to recognize that God is the one who provides for us. When Jesus tells us not to be anxious about what we eat or drink, it is because God knows what need (Matt. 6:32).

- The second rule for spiritually responsible eating is the rule of gratefulness. Recognizing that God knows what we need gives us the freedom to be grateful for what we receive. Jesus set the pattern for this by giving thanks whenever He ate with the disciples.

- A third way we can eat responsibly is by being generous. It is reasonable to provide food for ourselves. But we should not think of ourselves alone. James 2:15–16 says, "Suppose a brother or a sister is without clothes and daily food. If one of you says to them, 'Go in peace; keep warm and well fed,' but does nothing about their physical needs, what good is it?" This kind of selfish disregard epitomizes what James calls "dead" faith. One of the ways we express our gratefulness to God for His provision is to "remember the poor" by making provision for them. You might contribute to a rescue mission or volunteer at the community's food pantry.

Every ordinary meal is a complement to the Lord's Supper. The church's supper is a sacred meal. Its observance is set apart from ordinary eating (1 Cor. 11:22, 26–31). Our observance of the Lord's Supper reminds us of Jesus, who is the bread from heaven and who has provided us with eternal life (John 6:33, 41, 48, 50). He is more necessary for our life than any ordinary food or drink. Because He came to give His body and shed His blood for our salvation, He called His flesh "real food" and His blood "real drink" (John 6:55).

Yet the elements that make up the Lord's Supper are common in their origin. They do not come from heaven like Jesus but are prepared by human hands. The context of the Lord's Table elevates these ordinary elements into something extraordinary. At the same time, the sacred table dignifies the human work that was necessary to provide the food and the human hands that placed it there. In the process, it elevates all common work. "Everything we make is a loaf, formed to be broken, distributed, shared. We work to meet practical needs but not only that," theologian Peter Leithart observes. "We build for beauty, cook for taste, shape stone, and smear paint to give visual pleasure. The

Eucharist reminds us that we transform creation in order to make a delightful world more delightful."[9]

Every common meal anticipates the greater celebration that awaits us in the kingdom (Matt. 26:29; Rev. 19:9). In this way, our daily bread orients us in sacred time by pointing us to the hope that awaits us, and by reminding us in the here and now that heaven intersects earth at every point. The words of a popular wall hanging capture this truth despite its Hallmark sentiment. Jesus Christ really *is* the head of the home, the unseen guest at every meal, and the silent listener to every conversation. But He is more than an invisible presence; by the Holy Spirit, Christ is an active participant in the small details of my life. Whether we eat or drink or in whatever we do, it is an opportunity to glorify God (1 Cor. 10:31).

The day after I graduated from high school, I went to stay in a mountain cabin in the hills of Pennsylvania with three of my friends. It was a rustic setting without running water or indoor plumbing. The place had an old wood-burning stove that filled the cabin with smoke when it was lit. Our meal plan for the summer was a simple one. One of my friends was serious about his macrobiotic diet. Interested in Asian culture, he planned to major in Japanese in college. But it wasn't just the food that attracted him to the diet; it was the philosophy that came with it. He was attracted to a worldview that emphasized the importance of a balanced life and saw eating as an essential element in the fabric of that life. The rest of us weren't interested in the philosophical aspects at all. We were just looking for a cheap way to survive the summer.

Our resolve to live on brown rice and vegetables lasted for only a few days. One evening on our way back from a trip to town to do our laundry, we saw a sign for Kentucky Fried Chicken. It didn't take much to persuade us to turn in. If I am remembering correctly, it was actually his idea. He later abandoned his macrobiotic lifestyle altogether. But he was right about one thing. There is more to eating than food.

Chapter 5

The Art of Being Self-Conscious

My dog, Gidget, does not worry about the future. Although she seems to have some sense of time—or at least seems to know when I am usually due home from work—she does not think about the future either. She can feel pain and, if the furious wagging of her tail is any evidence, the canine equivalent of happiness as well. She is conscious. But she is not self-conscious in the same way that I am. I suspect she has never wondered whether her life as a dog has purpose. She does not worry about death. She does not make plans. Life as a church leader could not be more different. Pastors and leaders live in a world of strategies, five-year plans, and vision statements.

Unlike theirs, my dog's life unfolds entirely in the present. If she has a sense of the future, it extends only as far as the next few moments. She looks forward to the cookie that I will toss her when she comes in from outside. But she does not wake up in the morning and think about what she will do in the evening. She is not planning her day tomorrow. Even if she could, she would not ask me to mark an important date on the calendar. Gidget seems to exist entirely in the present tense.

Yet her experience is not what I mean by living life in the here and now. Practicing the present does not mean that we live our lives with a kind of animal immediacy, thinking only of what we need or desire in the moment. It is not reactive living that responds to whatever stimulus I happen to be experiencing in the moment without reflection. Christian living in the present tense demands a kind of self-consciousness that is guided by the Holy Spirit and filtered by the truth of God's Word. It is a reflection of my capacity to act as a volitional being created in the image of God.

The Virtue of Being Self-Conscious

This may come as a surprise. We do not usually think of self-consciousness as a virtue. It is a trait of an awkward soul. Our image of the self-conscious person is one of shuffling timidity. It is the aspect of someone who has no confidence but is nevertheless self-absorbed. The self-conscious person is one who is continually engaging hand-wringing and apology. Even worse, self-consciousness seems to us to be the path that leads to unhealthy introspection, if not to outright narcissism. One Christian author who writes on the subject of sanctification, for example, seems to suggest that the path to holiness is to think less about ourselves, not more: "What we need then is not more and more introspection (in a world chock-full of 'selfies,' we are already too myopic), but to fix our gaze steadfastly on Christ."[1] Similarly, in his classic treatment on the subject of spiritual depression, Martyn Lloyd-Jones affirms the practice of self-examination but warns against self-centered introspection. "I suggest that we cross the line from self-examination to introspection when, in a sense, we do nothing but examine ourselves, and when such self-examination becomes the main and chief end in our life," he writes. "We are meant to examine ourselves periodically, but if we are always doing it . . . that is introspection."[2]

We are suspicious of introspection because we associate it with the kind of navel-gazing that is characteristic of Eastern mysticism. Are we really supposed to sit on a mat and think about ourselves? Such an approach seems to be looking in the wrong direction, especially for Christians who are oriented toward doing. We suspect it would be better to turn the focus away from ourselves. Besides, the personality profile of many church leaders leans in the direction of activism. We would prefer to be busy about the Lord's work (and getting others busy) or at least engaged in prayer rather than spending extended periods of time thinking about ourselves.

There seems to be some truth in this. After all, wasn't the first aftereffect of sin mentioned in Genesis really a form of self-awareness? "Then the eyes of both of them were opened, and they realized they were naked; so they sewed fig leaves together and made coverings for themselves" (Gen. 3:7). The eyes of Adam and Eve were opened to themselves and their first reaction was to take cover. To us, it looks as if their vision had shifted away from God to themselves. It is no accident that since ancient times, the church has considered pride to be chief among all the capital sins. It has been called the queen of all sins and is identified as the sin that caused Satan to fall (see 1 Tim. 3:6). Self-absorption is the essence of pride.

Elsewhere in Scripture, we read that we must be intentional, turning our gaze away from ourselves: "Do nothing out of selfish ambition or vain conceit. Rather, in humility value others above yourselves, not looking to your own interests but each of you to the interests of the others" (Phil. 2:3–4). Some of the things Paul says about himself make it sound as if he was especially adverse to the idea of dwelling upon himself, especially when it came to his own ministry. "I care very little if I am judged by you or by any human court; indeed, I do not even judge myself" he asserts to those in Corinth who were scrutinizing his ministry (1 Cor. 4:3). Late in the same book, he tells the church, "No one should seek their own good, but the good of others" (1 Cor. 10:24). The message seems clear. Stop thinking about yourself so much. Put the book down. Go do something for somebody else.

Biblically Informed Introspection

But if we think carefully about what Genesis 3:7 reveals about the reaction of Adam and Eve, we realize that the destructive consequence of sin was not that they became aware of themselves, but rather the opposite. The consequence of sin was that they were no longer comfortable with themselves. Sin does not make us inclined toward introspection but the opposite. It blinds us to our true selves. It makes our own self-company insufferable. We do not want to dwell upon ourselves; we want to cover ourselves. Especially when we realize that we are in the presence of God.

There is indeed a connection between our discomfort with the idea of intentional self-consciousness and sin. But it is not the one we thought. The practice of self-awareness inevitably makes us aware of the reality of our own sinfulness. Not only do we become aware of who we are as God created us; we also become painfully aware of how that has been corrupted. In one of his journal entries, John Wesley described an encounter with a man after he had preached. As Wesley was leaving, a man caught hold of him and demanded to speak with him. "I must speak with you and will," the man said. "I have sinned against light and against love. I have sinned beyond forgiveness. I have been cursing you in my heart and blaspheming God ever since I came here. I am damned. I know it. I feel it in my heart. I am in hell. I have hell in my heart."[3]

Martyn Lloyd-Jones is right to warn us about the danger of morbid introspection. There is sufficient reason for us to be disheartened when we see ourselves apart from the grace of God and the redeeming work of Jesus Christ. Paul's assessment of himself where sin was concerned was stark: "For I know that good itself does not dwell in me, that is, in my sinful nature" (Rom. 7:18). It's no wonder we shy away from self-knowledge. The vision of ourselves in our true light is overwhelming. Anyone who has even glimpsed such a vision will understand Paul's cry in Romans 7:24: "What a wretched man I am! Who will rescue me from this body that is subject to death?" Like Adam we are shamed by the naked truth where sin is concerned.

Any practice of self-conscious introspection that is not informed by both the truth of God's Word and the hope of the gospel can only move in two directions. Either it will lead us in the direction of denial, so that we persuade ourselves that we are better than we really are. Or it will move in the direction of shame and despair. Introspection alone does not necessarily lead to a genuine self-understanding. Genuine self-understanding in turn does not always lead to hope. C. S. Lewis had his imaginary demon Screwtape urge Wormwood to deploy the practice of self-examination as a temptation strategy. "Keep his mind on the inner life," Screwtape counsels Wormwood regarding his subject. "He thinks his conversion is something *inside* him and his attention is therefore chiefly turned at present to the states of his own mind—or rather to that very expurgated version of them which is all you should allow him to see."[4] Even when we think we are self-aware, we may be hiding the worst from ourselves.

The psalmist asked God to search him and "see" if there was any offensive way in him (Ps. 139:24). The psalmist understood the danger. He did not trust his own vision in these matters. We often hide our true motives even from ourselves. We find it easy to look away from what would otherwise be a glaring inconsistency if we saw it in someone else. Sometimes the more horrible the reality, the easier it is for us to ignore it. No wonder Screwtape advised Wormwood: "You must bring him to a condition in which he can practise self-examination for an hour without discovering any of those facts that about himself which are perfectly clear to anyone who has ever lived in the same house with him or worked in the same office."[5]

The Mitigating Factor of God's Grace

Yet grasping the truth about ourselves may not leave us any better off. Without the mitigating factor of God's grace, any genuine self-awareness will show us what we are but without any hope for change. We will look into our hearts and see hell there. The practice that I am recommending is not morbid self-reflection. Neither is it a matter of putting the best face on a bad situation. Those who are in leadership may struggle with both tendencies but are probably most inclined toward the latter. We know that others tend to place us on a pedestal. We would prefer to stay on the pedestal in order to preserve our image as a strong leader. But the pedestal-bound leader is not who we truly are.

It is the practice of biblically directed self-reflection that enables us to see who we are in Jesus Christ. It also helps us to understand our personality and nature. Interestingly, while Martyn Lloyd-Jones discouraged introspection, he affirmed the importance of self-awareness. "Here, then, is the point at which we must always start. Do we know ourselves?" he observed. "Do we know our own particular danger? Do we know the thing to which we are particularly subject?"[6]

The *Confessions of Saint Augustine*, one of the greatest works of Christian literature, is an extended exercise in self-reflection. For Augustine, who was a church leader himself, this was an inward journey that was undertaken as an act of worship. He was not engaging in morbid self-interest but was looking for God. It was a journey that required courage. Augustine knew full well that what he would find when he turned his vision inward would not be pretty. "I will now call to mind my past foulness, and the carnal corruptions of my soul: not because I love them, but that I may love Thee, O my God," Augustine writes.[7]

Augustine's inward journey was tremendously influential in the West, not only because of its impact on Christian spirituality, but because of its effect on the secular world. Both turned inward but for different reasons. Augustine was looking for God. The secular philosophers who followed him were looking for themselves. Augustine was looking for himself, too. But only because he knew that he had been pursued by God. This is why Augustine's inward journey did not confine itself to the here and now. Much of what he wrote about had to do with his personal history. Augustine was not afraid to explore this dark territory because he knew his own story. He knew that he would meet God there.

Once again, we find that practicing the present does not

mean that we must disregard the past. This is especially true when it comes to introspection. When we engage in introspection, it is inevitable that the past will come to mind. An analogy from the realm of physics may help us to understand why. Sir Isaac Newton's first law of motion says that an object at rest stays at rest and an object in motion continues with the same speed and in the same direction unless acted upon by an unbalanced force. This is why you wear seat belts in your car. If the car unexpectedly becomes an object at rest, say by running into an immovable object in front of you, everybody in the car continues with the same speed and in the same direction.

Introspection affects us in a similar way. When we stop and engage in self-conscious introspection, we continue to feel the momentum of all that preceded that moment. This is why our initial experience may be unsettling instead of peaceful. In a sense, our minds and our lives are still in motion. The jumble of thoughts and worries, that have been stirred up by the turbulence of our lives comes rushing into that quiet space and we can't help feeling like we should move with it. We may be distracted at first and agitated. We feel like we should *do* something. If we are determined to be still and wait for the disorder to settle down, we soon discover something else. We have been in motion because we have been busy but that is not the only reason. Those who wait out the initial storm often realize that they have been in motion because we have been in flight. Perhaps it is a flight from ourselves. It may be a flight from God. Usually, it is a combination of both. As the dust settles in that quiet space of reflection, we begin to see those aspects of our-selves and our lives that we have been trying to keep at bay.

For me, this usually happens at night, when I am forced to stop moving. I lie down to sleep, but the momentum of the day continues. I rewind the events of the past day and watch them again, evaluating my performance. I am like an athlete watching a video of the game that just ended. I criticize my actions. I replay my conversations, improving my responses with all the things I *should* have said when I had the chance. After I have sorted through all the remains of the day, I turn my attention to the more distant past and begin to sift through my memories like an archeologist looking for clues. From there, I project into the future with the past as my template. Will it get better? Will it be worse?

I am not alone in this. The intersection of the past and future at the point of the present is a pattern we often find in the Psalms. But the psalmist does more than simply review the past and speculate about the future. The psalmist ponders the reality of God's presence in all three spheres (see Ps. 77:3–12). He begins by dwelling on God's faith-fulness to him in the past and from there projects into the future based upon his present dilemma: "Will the Lord reject forever? Will he never show his favor again? Has his unfailing love vanished forever? Has his promise failed for all time? Has God forgotten to be merciful? Has he in anger withheld his compassion?" the psalmist asks (vv. 7–9). These questions sound like a challenge, and they are. But it is a challenge aimed at the psalmist himself.

Directing Our Gaze toward God

The psalmist intentionally directs his gaze toward God. This is an exercise of the intellect. It is an exercise in reasoning. He does not blank his mind in an effort to unite with God's essence. He argues with himself and takes stock of the facts. "This is what my situation is," he says. "This is what God has done in the past. Is it really possible that He will deal differently with me in the future?" The implied answer to the psalmist's question is no. This sounds like it could be a pep talk, and in a way, it is. But it is more. It is the psalmist's attempt to detect God's presence.

Several years ago, I visited the Civil War battlefield in Gettysburg, Pennsylvania. As we walked the grounds, I noticed that there were photographs displayed throughout the park. Some things had changed. The people in the pictures were gone. They had died long ago. But the basic features of the landscape were still the same. I recognized the same rolling hills and the same great boulders portrayed in the faded photographs. The recognition sent shivers down me. Suddenly this historic battle no longer seemed like an artifact of history. It was as if what was past had somehow been transported into the present. Something similar happens for the psalmist as he traces the lines of God's faithfulness onto the landscape of his present experience. As he surveys the future, he expects those features to remain. The circumstances may change, but God's presence will remain the same. When we engage in this kind of introspection, we are trying to do the same. We are examining the landscape of the present to find the recognizable features of God's presence in our lives.

If it makes us uncomfortable to call this form of practicing the present introspection, we might feel better if we think of it as contemplation. A change of terms will not make some of us any more comfortable with the idea, especially those who live in the busy world of the church leader. To many of us, it is the language of the cloister. Contemplation seems to us to be a luxury afforded only to those who have nothing else to do. But perhaps we are wrong in holding such assumptions. Eugene Peterson offers a simpler and more practical description of what is involved. "Contemplation means submitting to the biblical revelation, taking it within ourselves, and then living it unpretentiously, without fanfare," he explains. "It doesn't mean (and these are the stereotyped misunderstandings) quiet, withdrawn, secluded, serene, or benign."[8] According to Peterson, you can be a mechanic, child, or even a pastor and engage in contemplative reflection.

According to theologian Josef Pieper, the practice of contemplation has three important elements. The first is "a silent perception of reality."[9] Contemplation is reflective by nature. It is quiet work that must usually be carried out in silence. It is not something that can be done on the run. If we are going to engage in contemplation, we must carve out enough time for it. Since it is silent work, it normally requires a certain kind of space. The circumstances do not have to be extreme. You don't need to live in a cave. But you should find a quiet and comfortable place that is as free as possible from distraction. Turn off the telephone and the television. The coffee shop is probably not the best spot for this sort of work.

According to Pieper, the second element that is involved in contemplation is what he calls intuition. He calls this "knowledge of what is actually present" and compares it to the experience of the physical senses, particularly the sense of seeing.[10] In other words, contemplation involves more than a rational analysis of our circumstances. What is involved here is hard to put into words. It is an experience of knowing that is rooted in the present. It is a form of seeing that is combined with being. We all know what it is like to be in a situation without really "being" there. We are present in the circumstance but not really present in our own experience. Our attention is divided, perhaps because our mind is elsewhere. Or maybe it is a defense mechanism designed to create a sense of distance between ourselves and whatever is going on. We engage in a form of denial by recasting the situation in our mind.

Contemplation involves knowing by experience. It is a kind of knowing that takes place in the moment and springs up unbidden as a result of this experience. "Contemplation, then, is intuition; that is to say, it is a type of knowing which does not merely move toward its object but already rests in it," Pieper explains. "The object is present—as a face or a landscape is present to the eye when the gaze 'rests upon it.'"[11] Because of this experiential dimension, the practice of contemplation often begins with the ordinary and physical. It begins by taking note of your surroundings. You might begin by making yourself aware of the room you are in with its ordinary furniture. There is the hum of the air conditioner in the background and the buzz of a fly tapping against the window. You can hear your own breathing, soft and regular as you sit quietly. You are choosing to be exactly where you are. Do not expect your experience at this point to be transcendent. That is not the intent. The goal is to focus our minds and our senses on the immediate. It is to enter fully into the present.

In his directions to those who are just learning to pray, Anthony Bloom describes a process that is similar to this. Bloom first directs his pupils to find a location with minimal distractions and to take note of their surroundings. "Try to find time to stay alone with yourself: shut the door and settle down in your room at a moment when you have nothing else to do," Bloom explains. "Say 'I am now with myself', and just sit with yourself."[12] Bloom warns that the first thing we will probably experience is boredom. This should tell us something about why we find it hard to practice the present. We do not really enjoy our own company. This is the first task for those who want to practice the presence by engaging in contemplative introspection. We will need to learn how to be present with ourselves. We will need to start small and work our way up. Half an hour is probably too much. Pastors enjoy advantages and disadvantages when it comes to this. On one hand, most pastors enjoy the advantage of managing their own schedules. They do not punch a clock. They can schedule time for contemplation into their day without much difficulty.

The disadvantage that pastors face, however, is that they are often too distracted by the many tasks that they have to accomplish—such as sermon preparation, meetings, counseling—to make the time for contemplation.

This sounds like too big a project, especially for those of us who aren't introverts. Ten minutes might even be too much. One strategy that Bloom recommends for addressing this problem is to redeem "crumbs of wasted time" and practice this in short bursts. "If you think of the number of empty minutes in a day when we will be doing something because we are afraid of emptiness and of being alone with ourselves, you will realize that there are plenty of short periods which could belong to both us and to God at the same time."[13] We might call this a spiritual reality check. It is simply a matter of acknowledging the reality of our surroundings, atmosphere, and ourselves.

THE SIXTY-SECOND CONTEMPLATIVE

In the 1980s, Ken Blanchard wrote *The One Minute Manager*. Other books followed that showed how people could tackle difficult and time-consuming tasks by focusing on them for sixty-second intervals. Perhaps someone should write a book called *The One Minute Contemplative*. Although contemplation usually requires time and solitude, we don't need to quit our jobs and live in a cave to be contemplative. If you find time and privacy hard to come by, remember that God is as present in a crowded room or busy workplace as He is in an empty sanctuary.

Identify cues in your busy day that remind you to stop for sixty seconds and practice the presence of God. This may be something you do several times throughout the day, like getting a cup of coffee or opening a file drawer. Use the action as a reminder to check in with God for a few moments. Do you sense the prompting of His Spirit in some way? When you set the table for dinner, take sixty seconds to consider that God likewise prepares a table for us even in the worst of circumstances (Ps. 23:5). The cues you select should be simple and repeated.

Scripture is an especially helpful tool for sixty-second contemplation. Pick a verse that seems especially suited to your circumstances and write it down. Spend sixty seconds thinking about it at strategic points in your day.

The third element of contemplation involves a kind of recognition or awareness. Pieper writes, "Traditionally, contemplation has been characterized as a knowing accompanied by amazement."[14] This language may be problematic for us, especially if we are only beginners who are struggling with this discipline. To speak of amazement sounds as if our aim in practicing the present is to achieve some kind of beatific vision or ecstatic experience. What if we find instead that our attempts are met with something less? Our attention wanders down the paths of the past or the future and we find that we must reign it in. At the end of our first few attempts, we likely are not met with a glorious vision of God but with the dismay of realizing how long five short minutes can seem.

Contemplation as Alignment

Maybe it would be helpful if we used other language to describe this third element. The amazement that Pieper speaks of is really a kind of alignment of vision so that we see things as they really are—and as God sees them. It is the sort of recognition that the psalmist describes in Psalm 73. Before the change, he had nearly lost his foothold because of the prosperity of the wicked. They do not seem to be bothered by the same afflictions that trouble the righteous. The wicked have no regard for God but appear to be carefree and succeed beyond measure. A superficial assessment of his circumstances caused the psalmist to conclude, "Surely in vain I have kept my heart pure and have washed my hands in innocence" (v. 13). The turning point came when he entered the sanctuary and engaged in contemplation: "When I tried to understand all this, it troubled me deeply till I entered the sanctuary of God; then I understood their final destiny" (vv. 16–17). His circumstances had not changed, but his vision did. By tracing God's larger design on the field of his experience, the psalmist gained a very different perspective.

The psalmist's experience is a helpful reminder that this work of contemplative introspection is not limited to those times when we feel good about God or our circumstances. It is a discipline for times in the valley as well as for those on the mountaintop. Our problem with practicing contemplative introspection in the valley is not the questions that plague us but the danger that we will do so dishonestly. We will come wearing a mask instead of showing up as our true selves. Instead of taking stock of things as they really are, we will engage in premature apologetics and attempt to explain away our pain, doubt, or difficulty.

In Psalm 73:21–22, the psalmist describes how his perspective changed: "When my heart was grieved and my spirit embittered, I was senseless and ignorant; I was a brute beast before you." This was a hard lesson to learn, but it was essential if he was to grasp the wonder of his real situation: "Yet I am always with you; you hold me by my right hand. You guide me with your counsel, and afterward you will take me into glory" (vv. 23–24). The counterpoint between his blind ignorance of the reality of his situation compared with God's unfailing commitment and faithful guidance would not have been possible if he had not begun with the stark honesty described in the first half of the psalm.

In contemplation, we do not try to work ourselves into a state of spiritual bliss. We do not need to elevate our feelings or put a good face on our bad mood. It is important as we begin to simply take note of things as they are without rendering judgment. Simply notice; do not evaluate. *This is where I am. This is how I feel.* It is especially important to do this when we are practicing the discipline of contemplative introspection in times of suffering, doubt, and discouragement. "This means calling the feelings we know by their correct names," Pierre Wolff observes in a book with the intriguing title *May I Hate God?* "I must face myself as I am. If I am angry, I must recognize this. If I hate, I must not hide what I feel from myself or the Father and call it by some nice name."[15]

Owning up to our anger, hate, and disappointment is all part of owning the present. To do otherwise is not only dishonest but dangerous. Wolff points out that such deception ignores the obvious. It is only when we show the doctor our wounds that we can be treated. But more than this, ignoring what is really true about me closes the door to genuine communication. "This particular feeling pervades my whole life; everything is influenced by it," Wolff explains. "So it is probably the only springboard from which I can leap to the Lord."[16] Or perhaps better, the broken landscape of my true feelings, as disappointed as it may leave me with myself, is the only landscape where I can really find God. He is interacting with me in my real life, not in my fantasy life.

What is more, the psalmist's journey from brute ignorance to spiritual understanding shows that we do not need to start in the right place to gain spiritual understanding. Our practice of fearless introspection is grounded in the knowledge that God is unfailing in His love and relentless in His commitment to us. Even when we are at our worst,

God continues to pursue us. We may be horrified by the truth about ourselves, but He is not. At this point, we are the only ones in the dark about the true state of our own hearts.

We do not need to be spiritual giants to practice the present. Is it the spiritual work of ordinary people. The practice of contemplative introspection may rightly be the exercise of a Spirit-empowered self-consciousness. It involves a periodic taking stock of myself and my situation. It is the kind of healthy self-monitoring that enables me to respond to signals I send to myself and to those that others give me. But most of all it is a discipline that helps me to align my perspective with God's by tracing His presence on the landscape of the past, present, and future.

My dog, Gidget, does not worry about the future, but she does live in the present. She is concerned only with the here and now. This was the psalmist's problem too when he envied the prosperity of the wicked. "I was senseless and ignorant; I was a brute beast before you" (73:22), he later realized. He came to this realization only after engaging in a fearless self-assessment in the here and now. Faithful Christian living demands that we exercise a special kind of self-consciousness. This is not the kind of morbid introspection that is narcissistic and self-absorbed. It is an honest self-examination that is guided by God's Word and His Spirit. Only God can enable me to do this.

Chapter 6

Inspired Intuition

Watson Thornton was already serving as a missionary in Japan when he decided to join the Japan Evangelistic Band, an evangelistic mission that was founded in England in 1903. He decided to travel to the town where the organization's headquarters was located and to introduce himself to its leader. But just as he was about to get on the train, he felt a tug in his spirit that he took to be the leading of the Lord telling him to wait. He was puzzled but thought he should obey.

When the next train rolled into the station, Watson started to board but again felt that he should wait. When the same thing happened with the third train, Watson began to feel foolish. Finally, the last train arrived and once more Watson felt a check. "Don't get on the train," it seemed to say. Shaking his head as he watched the train unload its passengers, he thought, *I guess I was wrong about this*. Watson thought he had wasted most of the day at the station for no apparent reason. Yet as he turned to go, he heard a voice call out his name. It was the mission leader he had intended to see. He came to ask whether Watson would consider joining the Japan Evangelistic Band. If Watson had ignored the impulse and boarded the train, he would have missed the meeting.

What was the impulse that made Watson wait at the station most of the day? He believed it was the voice of the Lord. Despite this, Watson felt unsure of himself. His actions certainly didn't seem to make sense at the time. What he was doing seemed to be more a matter of intuition than anything else.

A Flash of Insight

Someone has called intuition the inner voice that tells the thinking mind what to do next. Intuition is that flash of insight that prompts us to act in the moment. We all have had some experience with this. You feel a strong urge to call someone you haven't talked to in ages. When they answer the phone, they say, "I was just thinking about you." Or you are planning to depart for your road trip at a certain time but decide to leave two hours early. Later you learn that you missed a major traffic jam. Was it coincidence or guidance?

Some people think a sense of intuition can be developed and strengthened. Author Anne Lamott believes that all of us experience intuition but unlearn it during childhood: "When we listened to our intuition when we were small and then told grown-ups what we believed to be true, we were often either corrected, ridiculed, or punished."[1] We can get it back but not until we learn to trust our inner voice again. "You get your intuition back when you make space for it, when you stop the chattering of the rational mind," she explains. "The rational mind doesn't nourish you. You assume that it gives you the truth, because the rational mind is the golden calf that this culture worships, but this is not true."[2]

Well, that may be good advice for creatives. After all, Lamott is talking to writers. How much damage can you do by typing words onto a page? But it doesn't seem like a realistic philosophy for ordinary people. We can't just live by our intuition can we? It certainly seems unwise for Christians. Scripture warns that the heart is deceitful above all things (Jer. 17:9). How can we trust it? And the mind does not seem to fare much better. Proverbs 3:5–6 advises, "Trust in the LORD with all your heart and lean not on your own understanding; in all your ways submit to him, and he will make your paths straight." We can't trust our heart or our mind. What is there left to guide us?

There is the Bible, of course. But it often does not speak to us with the kind of specificity we might desire. It certainly works well enough on the big things. Don't commit adultery. Don't murder. Make disciples of all nations. Be responsible in your work. Yet it doesn't speak about the fine details in these matters. To which church should I accept a call as pastor? What week should we schedule vacation Bible school this year? Should our short-term missions team go to Mexico or Uganda this year? There are all kinds of decisions that I have to make that cannot be made by turning to a specific chapter and verse. The Bible will tell me what my married life ought to look like, but it won't give me the name of the person to whom I should propose. It provides guidelines that enable me to be a good employee, but it won't tell me whether I should work for IBM or McDonald's.

We *do* see something like intuition at work in the lives of God's people in the Bible. Abraham packs up his family and leaves Ur of the Chaldeans. When they ask where he is headed, he says that he doesn't know. Yet he's not going nowhere. Abraham is on his way to the land that God will show him (Gen. 12:1). The Shunammite woman whose son had been raised from the dead by Elisha returns from exile after seven years and decides to go to the king to beg for her house and land back. She happens to arrive just as Elisha's servant Gehazi is telling her story (2 Kings 8:5). Paul tries to enter Asia but is "kept by the Holy Spirit" from doing so (Acts 16:6). He tries to enter Bithynia but his progress is checked by "the Spirit of Jesus" (v. 7). He passes by Mysia and goes down to Troas where he has a vision of a Macedonian man begging him to come and help them (v. 9). Paul took this as a call from God and got ready at once to leave.

Suprarational Decision-Making

Acting on intuition seems as if it is relying on the irrational or at least some nonrational part in us. However, it might be better to describe it as suprarational. It involves thinking, but there is more to it than that. An intuitive act does not entirely skirt the rational processes since it often involves a decision. But it is one that is made based on different criteria than we usually rely upon when deciding or acting. Intuitive acts seem nonconscious because they don't usually involve long deliberation. We do not go through a list of pros and cons or engage in exhaustive research. Instead, the decision is made or the action taken in a moment.

Intuitive acts are more holistic than those that are purely rational. They seem to come from some place deep within. They are decisions made by the whole self rather than just the mind. Those who act on intuition often say that they are acting on the gut or their instinct. They cannot explain how they know what they should do; they just know that it is the right thing to do. It is still rational in the sense that the mind is engaged. Intuitive actions are carried out without forethought or deliberation. They take place in a moment, but they are not unconscious. We do not go into a trance. Our faculties are not possessed by a higher power, so that we no longer have to worry about using our own strength. There is a decision made or an action taken. Yet it is not by the same deliberative process we typically engage in when choosing or acting. The speed is also different. Many times intuitive actions take place in an instant. They are done before we know what we have done. They are more effective than intellectual. Those who act on intuition feel more than think about what they are doing.

Although the processes behind intuition seem mysterious, they may just be hidden. David G. Myers, a social psychologist at Hope College, observes: "Today, cognitive science is revealing a fascinating unconscious mind that Freud never told us about: Thinking occurs not onstage but offstage, out of sight."[3] It is probably not a question of one or the other but both. "Thinking, memory and attitude operate on two levels: the conscious/deliberate and the unconscious/automatic. 'Dual processing' researchers call it. We know more than we know we know."[4]

There is an additional factor where God's people are concerned. In addition to whatever natural processes are involved in intuitive actions, believers often act based on what might be called "inspired" intuition. They are moved not only by the unseen processes that effect everyone else but by the Holy Spirit. This was how Paul understood his decision not to enter Asia, Bithynia, or Mysia. The influence of the Spirit was what compelled Watson Thornton not to get on the train, even though that was what he had come to the station to do. We usually describe this as following the "leading" of the Holy Spirit.

This is a sensitive subject for some Christians. One reason is we are not exactly sure how this guidance works. Even though there are clear instances in the Scriptures, the exact details are not always included, nor do they necessarily fit our experience. For example, we are told in Acts 13:2 that the church of Antioch was prompted by the Spirit to commission Paul and Barnabas and send them out on mission. In this case, the call did not come through some inner intuition but when the Holy Spirit spoke as the church was fasting and worshiping. But just how did the Sprit speak? The explicit mention of prophets and teachers could suggest that there was some kind of prophetic directive. Yet the text does not actually say this. Perhaps the group as a whole came to see that this was what God wanted. We know the outcome, but we don't know the specifics.

The same is true of the directions Paul received while he was on his missionary journey. We know that the Spirit directed him not to enter some regions and allowed him to enter others. But apart from the one vision, we really don't know what form this direction took. Was it a "feeling" on Paul's part that some destinations were just not right? Did God use obstacles and circumstances to nip at Paul's heels like a sheepdog in order to guarantee that he ended up in the right place at the right time? In the end, Paul was directed to his destination by a vision. Yet his extraordinary experience does not seem to reflect the normal experience of the majority of us. In our case, the Spirit seems to carry out His ministry of guidance by employing more ordinary means. Instead of being visited by a prophet, we receive an email or a phone call inviting us to apply for a pastoral position. When trying to decide which youth pastor to hire, the choice is made when one of them turns us down. The processes we use are not at all extraordinary, but that does not mean that God is not in them.

Led by the Spirit

Just as we do not entirely understand the natural processes that are involved when we act intuitively, we do not always know the spiritual processes that are involved when God directs us as believers. We often talk about being "led" by the Lord, but when Paul employs this language in Galatians 5:18, he is talking about morality not decision-making. Those who are led by the Spirit are empowered by Him to obey. They "walk"—that is, live—by the Spirit and do not gratify the desires of the flesh, the sinful nature. Being led by the Spirit in a biblical sense is not the art of spontaneous direction or action but the power of God to obey. New Testament scholar F. F. Bruce explained, "To be 'led by the Spirit' is to walk by the Spirit—to have the power to rebut the desire of the flesh, to be increasingly conformed to the likeness of Christ (2 Cor. 3:18), to cease to be under the law."[5] According to Bruce, to be "led by the Spirit" is synonymous with being under grace. This is why Paul elsewhere says that being led by the Spirit is one of the proofs that we belong to God (Rom. 8:14).

This is an important correction for a church that tends to evaluate its leaders on the basis of their gifts rather than their character. In recent days, we have seen many notable pastors come under criticism for abusive leadership and infidelity. It seems their behaviors were often known, but ignored or explained away by those around them. Such denials are misguided attempts to shield the church from pain. People refuse to accept the evidence that is presented to them because they do not want to face the implications that come with it. They reason that the ministry is too big to subject it to the consequences of such failure. Or they refuse to accept the evidence presented to them because they believe that a leader who could produce such ministry fruit could not possibly be guilty. Because many church leaders tend to be goal oriented, it is easy for them to be more interested in direction and results than in walking in holiness. We often gauge a church's success by its attendance figures rather than its character or its life.

Here, then, is the first principle when it comes to guidance for those who practice the present. You already know most of what you need to know to be where you are supposed to be. The art of being led by the Spirit is not a matter of waiting each moment for some mystical experience of divine direction. It is a matter of trusting God for the power to obey what He has already told you to do. Do you want to be led by the Spirit? Then do what God has already told you is right. Do it in the power of His Spirit.

The trouble with living by natural intuition is that it sometimes leads us astray. Some will say that our instincts are never wrong. We should always lead with our gut. But our actual experience proves otherwise. "It's true: Intuition is a big part of human decision-making," Myers notes. "But the complementary truth is that intuition often errs."[6] Research shows what our own experience tells us. Intuition is real, but it is not infallible. "Psychology, too, is replete with compelling examples of how people fool themselves," Myers explains. "Even the most intelligent people make predictable and costly intuitive errors; coaches, athletes, investors, interviewers, gamblers and psychics fall prey to well-documented illusory intuitions."[7]

What is more, the fact of the Holy Spirit's involvement in the believer's life does not mean that Christians are less prone to mistakes than ordinary people are. When I describe the believer's experience as "inspired" intuition, I am not using the term in its technical sense. The Bible does speak of inspiration, but it is in connection with the Holy Spirit's involvement in the formation of Scripture. The Greek word that is sometimes translated "inspired" in 2 Timothy 3:16 literally means "God breathed." This means that the Scriptures are the Word of God. Second Peter 1:21 uses the prophets as an example to describe the process by which God breathed out His Word through human instruments when it says that they were "carried along" by the Holy Spirit. Elsewhere this same term is used to speak of the driving wind of a storm. It is the language of control.

The Holy Spirit's unique work of inspiration guaranteed that the writers of Scripture would record only what God wanted to be written. As a result, we can be confident that all the Bible affirms to be true is indeed true. The Bible is infallible, but we are not. So when I speak of "inspired" intuition, I am using the term in a lower sense to speak of the immediacy and experiential dimension of the intuitive act. Biblical inspiration is unique and is limited to the authors of Scripture.

This raises an important question. If it is true that Christians can err just like anyone else when they act intuitively, then why should we listen to intuition at all? Doesn't the possibility that we might choose incorrectly render the practice of the present too risky? We must admit that there is a measure of risk. The intuitive choices made by Christians are not automatically better than those made by unbelievers.

Like that of everyone else, our hunches can and do go wrong. That investment that our gut told us would be good suddenly tanks. The employee we hired and with whom we seemed to have an instant connection turns out to be lazy. Our sudden impulse to call a friend results in a pleasant but insignificant conversation. We do not always get it right.

Yet the same is sometimes true of the decisions we make after long thought and careful deliberation. The fact that we sometimes get it wrong after doing our research and weighing all the pros and cons of a choice that we can think of does not cause us to conclude that we should throw reason and deliberation out the window. Why would we do the same with intuition? As a culture, we are biased toward nonintuitive thinking. We value reason and planning. Practicing the present does not mean that we replace deliberated decision-making with an approach that is purely intuitive. Leaders who practice the present learn to trust their Spirit-guided intuition. They are not afraid to make a decision in the moment when they sense God's prompting. It is worth the risk.

Why didn't God decide to use the Holy Spirit to give us an infallible understanding of the choices we have to make? I don't know. I do know that if He had, it would not have guaranteed our obedience. The Bible is full of instances in which God's people knew without a doubt what He wanted them to do and yet they chose to do otherwise. Infallible knowledge does not itself guarantee faithfulness of action. When Israel was poised on the border of Canaan, they did not need intuition to tell them where to go from there. Their problem was that their intuition sent them the wrong message. When they saw the size of the enemy, their gut reaction was: "We can't attack those people; they are stronger than we are" (Num. 13:31). Notice that this wasn't just intuition. It was also the result of their research. Yet Caleb's intuition sent the opposite message: "We should go up and take possession of the land, for we can certainly do it" (v. 30). What made the difference? Ultimately, it was a question of faith. Caleb's intuitive sense was shaped by God's promise.

God uses both careful deliberation and intuition to guide us. There is an element of risk in each. Our confidence is not in our own infallibility but in God's sovereignty. We know that if we belong to Jesus Christ, even when we get things wrong, all things work together for good (Rom. 8:28). This certainly does not mean that every decision we make is good. Nor does it mean that every outcome of the decisions we make will feel good. It does guarantee that God's ultimate plan for our lives cannot be thwarted, not even by our own missteps. Our plans will not always work out, but His plan will. His plan is that we will be conformed to the image of Jesus Christ (v. 29).

Assume God's Presence

So what does it look like when church leaders practice the present by tuning in to inspired intuition? It begins with assuming God's continuing and immediate presence. God's presence is mediated to believers in a unique way through the Holy Spirit. While everyone seems to have some capacity for intuition, what sets believers apart is their unique relationship to the Holy Spirit. Everyone can experience intuition, but only those who are in Christ can say that they are also indwelt by the Spirit (Rom. 8:9).

Too often, we relate to God as if He is far off and only drops in now and again to check up on us. We ignore God's presence, treating Him like an absent landlord. Our thoughts may turn to Him now and again, but we do not consider God to be our companion. We rarely take Him into account when we make decisions. Or we may be secretly convinced that God is ignoring us. Perhaps this is because we are convinced that we are insignificant and that the concerns of others are greater than our own. We suspect that we would need to do something extreme in order to attract God's attention.

Neither scenario is accurate. God is not an absentee landlord. Although the intrusion of sin into the world has made it difficult for us to sense the reality of His presence, God is still always and everywhere present with us. The psalmist marveled that there was no place that he could go to escape the reality of God's presence (Ps. 139:7–12). The universality of God's presence is situational as well as geographic. Just as there is no place we can go to escape from God, there is no circumstance we will ever find ourselves in that can separate us from His loving interest (Rom. 8:39–40).

God communicates the reality of His presence to us through the Holy Spirit. According to Romans 8:16, it is the Spirit who gives us the confidence to approach God on intimate terms. The Spirit is the seal on our adoption papers, the proof that we have been accepted by God as sons and daughters. The Holy Spirit reinforces in our experience the same truth that Jesus Christ taught by reassuring us that we are God's dear children. He helps us to address God as our Father rather than as our judge. We do not need to go to extreme measures to be assured of God's immediate presence in our lives. Nothing we can do will exceed what Jesus Christ has already done for us. His death and resurrection have guaranteed that we will be welcomed whenever we approach God and call Him by the familiar name of heavenly Father.

God's presence is the spiritual birthright of every believer. He is not more present with the church's leaders than He is with ordinary Christians. But leaders should take special comfort from the fact that Christ promised His presence in connection with the church's mission (see Matt. 28:20). The church's leadership task does not rest on our shoulders alone. Not only is Christ with us, He goes before us to prepare the way. He does not watch our efforts from a distance but is engaged with us as we lead.

Expect God's Guidance

God's acceptance of us would have little value if it did not also guarantee His interest in us. Some people may actually be unsettled by the thought of God as Father. Some fathers are emotionally detached. Some are abusive. Even the most interested father can sometimes seem aloof. When my sons were small, they loved to play with Legos. On many evenings after supper, I would get down on my hands and knees to help them with their Lego creations. I am a writer, not an architect or engineer. I have never been very good at building anything. But I did want to spend time with my sons, so I valiantly plunged my hand into the bucket of multicolored Lego blocks. It occurred to me that looking like I was building something was probably just as good as actually attempting to build something. So most evenings as they built, I sat and watched. Once in a while, I stirred the bucket, plucking out a few pieces and half-heartedly tried to fit them together. Years later, I asked my sons if they could tell what I was doing, and they both laughed. "We knew what you were up to, Dad," they said.

God does not lose interest in what we are doing. He is a Father who is always present and engaged. We can always expect His guidance. By that I mean we can expect that our lives will unfold according to a divine plan. Because we are moving in a direction that has been mapped out for us by Him, God is interested in its direction along with all its particular details. What is more, He has promised to guide us along the way. Anyone who lacks wisdom can ask for it, confident that their request will be granted (James 1:5). God does not merely stir the bucket; He has made the blueprint and is doing the building.

The promise of guidance does not necessarily mean that divine direction will come to us in some supernatural form. God is certainly capable of appearing to us in a burning bush, but He usually doesn't. We should not interpret this reticence as evidence of divine disinterest. It is just the opposite. God is always speaking to us. According to the psalmist, everything in creation speaks to us of His glory (Ps. 19). Eugene Peterson observed, "We live in a world, after all, in which God is supernaturally active, visibly and invisibly, both around and within us, far beyond our capacity to notice or explain, control or manage." Moreover, "It would be odd if we did not at least occasionally catch a glimpse of this 'beyond' in our backyards and remark on it—a sign, a sign of God's presence or work where we had not expected to see or hear it and in circumstances in which we cannot account for it."[8]

Furthermore, God *has* spoken to us. He has already given us plenty of proofs of His interest and detailed directions about how to live our lives: "In the past God spoke to our ancestors through the prophets at many times and in various ways, but in these last days he has spoken to us by his Son, whom he appointed heir of all things, and through whom also he made the universe" (Heb. 1:1–2). Guidance always begins with what God has already revealed. He will not contradict Himself. Whatever the nature of your immediate choice, start with the biblical principles that you already know apply to it.

Listen to Your Feelings

Till now, all that I have written in this chapter could apply to any kind of decision. One of the factors that sets intuitive action apart from deliberative action is its affective nature.

There is a reason intuitive decisions are often described as those made by the gut. The gut or bowels have traditionally been associated with feeling. In the Old Testament, the abdominal region was regarded as the seat of one's emotions (see Isa. 16:11). In the New Testament, the Greek term for bowels is associated with compassion (see Luke 10:33; Phil. 1:8; 1 John 3:17). When we act intuitively, we feel what is right before we know it is right. Or rather, we know what is right by the way that we feel. If you want to learn to act intuitively, you must learn how to listen to your feelings.

To listen does not mean that we automatically obey our feelings. Intuitive decision-making does not assume that our feelings always correspond with God's will. Sometimes the intuitive choice goes against what we desire. We know what we want but somehow we also know that what we want is the wrong thing. A few years into my pastoral ministry, I applied for a position at a church near my hometown. My wife, Jane, and I had wanted to return to the area since our seminary days. After graduating, I had tried to find a church there but had been unsuccessful. This congregation I was considering was larger than the one I was currently serving. It had multiple staff while I was the only pastor serving our congregation. It was close to family, almost within walking distance of the home where I grew up. Making the change also meant that we would be able to buy a house instead of living in a parsonage. Best of all, the church wanted me to come. All the signals pointed to a green light. All the signals, that is, except for one. There was a gentle whisper inside me that said it was the wrong thing to do. I wanted to go but I knew I had to say no. When the search committee asked for a reason, I could only tell them that it didn't seem like the Lord's will for me at the time.

An intuitive choice may actually be counterintuitive because it is the unexpected choice. Yet if the range of options before us falls within the broad scope of what God allows, more often than not the sensible thing is to do as you please. For the Christian, intuitive decision-making goes hand in hand with biblical understanding. The more I understand the larger framework of God's will as it is laid out for me in Scripture, the easier it is for me to trust the inclinations I have within the boundaries of that framework.

The Holy Spirit plays an essential role in a Christian model of intuitive thinking. I not only listen to my feelings, but also search my feelings on a regular basis to discern that tug that signals His direction. If we can expect God to guide us in our decisions, then it is also reasonable to expect that we will sense His direction. God's Spirit directs the mind but He also interacts with us in the affective realm. We can feel Him moving us toward one choice or another. The biblical data suggests that when this happens, it is subtle. Scripture describes God's voice as a gentle whisper (1 Kings 19:11–12). It is easily overlooked. If it feels like anything, it probably feels like a suggestion rather than a demand.

The more practiced we are in taking stock of our feelings, the more likely we are to discern the presence of God's voice. The more we make decisions based upon God's gentle whisper, the more confident we will be when the time comes to act upon His voice in the moment. In view of this, it is a good idea to practice listening. Acknowledge His presence and take stock of your feelings on a regular basis. Do you sense His voice? You don't need to wait until you have a major decision to make before listening for God's gentle whisper. Practice Spirit-driven intuition in the small choices as well as the large. In time you will more easily recognize the inner voice of God's Spirit and come to trust His guidance. Church leaders would do well to pause before making decisions to check for the gentle tug of God's Spirit. Are you inclined in a certain direction? Does it seem as if God's Spirit is also on board? In my experience, this is usually a negative test. If I am already inclined to move in a certain direction, I pause to see if there is a check in my spirit that signals the absence of the Holy Spirit's assent.

You will also come to trust God's intuitive guidance by paying attention to your failures as well as to your successes. We all have had moments when we felt like God wanted us to do something but didn't follow through. Afterward, we recognized that the impulse we ignored was the tug of God's Spirit. Sometimes this happens when we feel an urge to share the faith with someone but choose not to do so. Maybe we are in a hurry and don't want to take the time. Often it is because we are nervous about their response. Later on, we realize that God had set up a divine appointment, and we ignored it. Recalling those moments when we respond to God's prompting can be even more beneficial because past success will give us the courage to take the same risk in the future. In time, the tug of the Spirit grows more familiar and is easier to recognize.

In Scripture, intuitive action is a collective practice as well as an individual one. When the Holy Spirit directed Barnabas and Paul to embark on their missionary work from Antioch, He communicated this to the church as a whole (Acts 13:1–3). Likewise, although the vision that prompted Paul and his companions to go to Macedonia was given to Paul alone, the plural is used to speak of the actual decision to change direction (Acts 16:1–10; cf. vv. 6–7). The stereotype of the intuitive leader pictures a dynamic leader who functions as an oracle of God (for example, Moses). While this has sometimes been the case, the New Testament model of leadership seems to be more community oriented. Gifts are given to the whole church and each individual member contributes to the well-being of the whole. God does still speak to individual leaders but the community often ratifies that leader's sense of direction (Acts 6:5; 15:22, 25).

In today's leadership culture, listening to the voice of the community is sometimes viewed as the mark of an indecisive leader. The leaders we admire are top-down decision makers who cast vision and enlist support rather than those who listen for the voice of God speaking through others. This prophetic model is appealing because it seems more direct. The fewer people we involve in the decision loop, the less complicated the process—that is, until the time comes to implement the decision that was made. The leader-as-prophet model also appeals to our ego. In view of this, it is worth noting that the biblical prophets were usually outsiders. Prophet-leaders like Moses and David were rare. Most of Israel's kings needed the help of others to discern the will of God.

Of course, it could be argued that this was only because so many of them were disobedient. Perhaps if they had been more responsive to God, they would not have needed the prophets. But one of the most important distinctives of the church is that all those who are part of the body of Christ possess the Holy Spirit. The promise of the Spirit given to the church in Joel 2:27 and Acts 2:17 describes a universal outpouring of the Spirit on all of God's people. Not all believers are prophets, but all believers enjoy access to God's Spirit in a way that was once only true of prophets and a few select leaders in Israel.

How do leaders tap into the collective discernment of the larger body of Christ? It's not rocket science. Begin with a simple question: What do you think God wants us to do? Invite the church to engage in a season of listening prayer. Give them an opportunity to say what they believe the Spirit is directing the church to do and explain why they believe this is the case. You are not necessarily looking for unanimity, although this sometimes happens. Neither is this a call for a congregational vote. Leaders who invite the congregation into the decision-making process acknowledge a measure of uncertainty. They hope to hear the voice of God's Spirit in the voice of the congregation because they either do not know God's direction or are hoping to find confirmation for a direction they already sense.

Risk Being Wrong

We become more comfortable with intuitive action the more we practice it. However, given the subtle nature of this kind of direction and our own fallibility, we will sometimes misinterpret God's direction. The good news is that God is able to close doors as easily as He can open them. Some of the wrong choices we make by intuition may inconvenience us, but if we are acting in wisdom and in accordance with Scripture, they won't be catastrophic. Moreover, we can expect God to be involved in the process. Paul's mission from Antioch is a perfect example of this. Viewed from one angle, Paul's journey looks like one failed attempt after another. He thinks he should go to Asia, but he is wrong. From there, he decides to go to Bithynia, but is wrong again. It is only after he sees the vision that he knows where to go. Yet viewed from the perspective of God's direction, it is a testimony to His faithfulness. Whenever Paul began to move in the wrong direction, God was faithful in closing the door.

Our greatest fear, when it comes to God's guidance, is that we will get it wrong. We worry that we will turn right when God really wants us to go left. From that point on the trajectory of the rest of our lives will fall outside the will of God. This view makes God's direction seem like a secret that God has kept from us and that which we are obligated to discover on our own. God isn't going to tell us what the direction is, but if we get it wrong, then the rest of our life will be ruined. Leaders fear that they will miss the golden moment of opportunity and God's blessing in their ministry. Or worse, they will move the church in a direction that will end in disaster. They may lead the church down a blind alley or risk too much and hurt the church.

The view that it is entirely up to us to discover God's direction is inconsistent with the picture of the Holy Spirit's ministry that we find in the New Testament. The Holy Spirit is our guide and helper, who has been lovingly sent to us by Christ to be with us forever. He is the one who reminds us of God's truth (John 14:16, 26). When we misread God's direction, the Holy Spirit is always there to guide us to the right path. If we want to learn how to act on the basis of Spirit-directed intuition, we need to risk being wrong.

What should we do if we conclude that we have misread the signals? The answer depends on the nature of the decision. The greater the action, the greater the consequences. Often, the stakes are not very high. The most we suffer is loss of time, a certain amount of inconvenience, and the embarrassment of knowing that we were wrong. The stakes can be raised considerably if pride compels leaders to persist in the wrong direction. The first action that leaders should take when they determine they have missed God's cue and are moving in the wrong direction is openly admit that they have made a mistake. Don't gloss over the mistake. Avoid the temptation to shift blame. Speak the truth as simply and as clearly as you can. In most cases, the congregation will not be angry but relieved. You can be sure that many in the church will have already recognized the case or at least have strong reservations.

Once leaders have admitted that they are moving in the

wrong direction, they need to assess the situation before deciding what their next action should be. Is it possible to retrace your steps? A church that has added a second worship service can easily go back to one if they find that the new service isn't working out. A congregation that has embarked on a multimillion-dollar building project may find it more difficult to reverse their decision. Assessing the situation also involves taking stock of the moral and ethical commitments that are involved. Financial commitments should be honored if at all possible. Promises should be kept. When a commitment must be broken, there should also be an accompanying admission of error and apology. A curt statement that the church has decided to move in a different direction is not enough.

Leaders should expect God to continue to guide even when they have misread His direction. He will not abandon us. God's power is greater than our mistakes. In the end, it is the general trajectory of the journey that matters most and the destination is assured.

In the summer of 1988, Watson Thornton stopped at a post office in the small town of Green Valley, Illinois, to mail a package. He was in his eighties and retired after a long career in the ministry by then. He had moved to a nearby town to live with his daughter after his wife's death. Watson's first visit to Green Valley did not especially impress him. "The town does not even have a filling station for gasoline," he later observed. "I parked across the road from an old dingy storefront, with the title 'Valley Chapel' on it, and some children running out from their DV Bible School."

Despite its dingy appearance, Watson was interested in the tiny church. Two hours earlier, he had prayed, asking God if there might be a small country church nearby where he would feel comfortable. On an impulse, Watson crossed the street and walked in the door. "I stopped in and introduced myself to the young pastor, his wife, and some of the teachers," he later wrote. "They took me right in and I have felt very much at home."[9]

I know that this is true. I was the young pastor at the time.

If this was a miracle, it was a small one. Most people would probably write it off as a coincidence. What are the odds of finding a small country church in a town like Green Valley? Pretty good, I suppose. But to someone like Watson, who had spent his life listening for the gentle whisper of the Spirit, it was much more. It was a moment of inspired intuition. This was no coincidence, it was God's familiar voice—faithful in directing Watson in the small decisions, just as He had always been in the large ones.

Chapter 7

The Opportunity
of the Immediate

The Clock of the Long Now, also known as the millennium clock, is the vision of computer scientist Danny Hillis. He conceived it because he believes that one of our greatest problems has to do with our sense of time. We are too focused on the short-term. "Some people say that they feel the future is slipping away from them," he explains. "To me, the future is a big tractor-trailer slamming on its brakes in front of me just as I pull into its slip stream. I am about to crash into it."[1] The millennium clock is a real working clock whose components are being assembled in Seattle and California, while the clock itself is being built inside a mountain. The aim is to have a clock that will run for ten thousand years and will count time for millennia instead of hours.

Hillis envisioned a clock that would tick only once a year. Its century hand would move every hundred years, and a cuckoo would come out at each millennium. He sees the clock as an emblem of hope for the future. "I know I am a part of a story that starts long before I can remember and continues long beyond when anyone will remember me. I sense that I am alive at a time of important change, and I feel a responsibility to make sure that the change comes out well."[2]

At least two decades before Danny Hillis envisioned the millennium clock, Helmut Thielicke made a similar observation about our perspective of time. "There are no such things as round 'year-clocks' which begin afresh at number twelve after the passage of three hundred and sixty-five days," Thielicke remarked in a sermon on the subject of time and eternity. "We should have to visualise such a yearly chronometer differently; it would have to be a straight line on which every elapsed year was marked off as a small segment."[3] Thielicke argues, "Because our clocks are round, because the hands circle about and constantly return to their starting point, we acquire the illusion that everything in life repeats itself, that we can always make a fresh start."[4]

The Importance of the Here and Now

Hillis is right, of course. Our thinking is often in the short-term. Even when church leaders engage in long-term planning, it is really short-term as far as the future is concerned. Most leaders consider five to ten years to be long-term. This is a short time in the span of a lifetime and hardly noticeable when compared to eternity. Indeed, if we take the vast span of eternity into account, even the millennium clock is really just short-term. Danny Hillis is only thinking ahead for the next ten thousand years. Although the years seem long to us, we are only here for a brief moment: "They quickly pass, and we fly away" (Ps. 90:10). No wonder the psalmist prays that God would teach us to "number our days."

Thielicke is right, too. Our thinking tends to be cyclical where time is concerned. Pastors perform their work in cycles and seasons. They are looking ahead to the next date on the church calendar or ministry season. But they also know that once it has passed, it will roll around again. We are convinced that we have more time than we really do. What we don't get done today, we will be able to do tomorrow. A millennium clock or even the yearly clock that Thielicke imagines might make us think differently. We would have a sense that our life does not recycle each day but that instead we "creep along this line of time" and leave the past behind. "The hand never returns to where it was before. Once decisions are made we can never cancel them out."[5]

The long now is important, but so is the here and now. Our hope is indeed directed toward the future. Yet what happens in the future is often dependent on what we do with the present. Danny Hillis admits as much, at least by implication, when he cites the replacement of the oak beams in the ceiling of college hall at New College, Oxford, to illustrate the need for a millennium clock. "Last century, when the beams needed replacing, carpenters used oak trees that had been planted in 1386 when the dining hall was first built," Hillis explains. "The 14th-century builder had planted the trees in anticipation of the time, hundreds of years in the future, when the beams would need replacing. Did the carpenters plant new trees to replace the beams again a few hundred years from now?"[6] Probably not.

Every leader lives with the consequences of the day-to-day decisions that their predecessors made. Every pastor inherits not only the legacy of the previous pastor but of all the pastors that went before. Their values have been ingrained into the church's culture, not only by the big choices they made but also by thousands of small decisions and actions made on a daily basis. The long trajectory of a church's customs, expectations, and methods are set by the small actions its leaders make in the short-term.

Short-term thinking is the enemy of long-term thinking only when we don't take the long-term into account. We need both kinds. But there are times when we need *really* short-term thinking. There are times when we recognize that a singular opportunity has presented itself and we need to seize the moment. Acts 8 tells how Philip, a leader in the church at Jerusalem, introduced the gospel to the royal court of Ethiopia by sharing the gospel with one of the queen's officials on the Gaza road. He was directed to go there by an angel without being told why. If he had ignored the angel's prompting, Philip would have missed the appointment.

Many of the ministry opportunities that come to pastors and church leaders are like this. They are unplanned encounters. They almost seem like accidents. It may come in the form of a conversation we have in the coffee shop or a side remark made by someone as they are leaving the church. We may feel prompted to call on someone we haven't seen in church for a while or maybe it is an urgent prompting to pray for someone out of the blue. We usually don't have the luxury of being told what to do by an angel, but we do feel prompted by the Holy Spirit, who is an even higher authority. This is the opportunity of the immediate.

The opportunity of the immediate is rooted in a theology of divine interruption. It is the temporal dimension of inspired intuition discussed in the previous chapter. Because we often focus on our own grand designs for the future, we lose interest in the here and now. Since we are not attuned to the here and now, we miss the opportunity God places before us in the immediate moment. We are focused on the great thing that is going to happen next. God is doing something amazing right now but we are unable to see it. This often takes the form of focusing on structures and strategies instead of people. Leaders can be so concerned with plans, programs, and targets that they fail to notice the details of the work that God is doing right in front of them. We grieve over the fact that church attendance did not break the one hundred barrier and miss the fact that one person who did attend was profoundly affected by the message. We are so set on the big audacious goal we have set for the church that we are not paying attention to the hundreds of little goals that God is achieving on a daily basis.

One story in the Old Testament that has always haunted me is the brief account of the encounter of Israel's king Jehoash (or Joash) with the dying prophet Elisha in 2 Kings 13:13–19. The king came to visit Elisha because he had heard that he was ill. In fact, Elisha was on his death bed. But Jehoash wasn't only concerned for Elisha's health, he was worried about the future of the northern kingdom of Israel, which was being threatened by Syria. Jehoash was not a good king in the moral sense, but he had experienced some military success. He was hoping that Elisha could help him extend his success. The prophet's response was to require the king to perform two symbolic acts. First, he told Jehoash to get a bow and some arrows and take the bow in his hands. The prophet placed his hands over the king's on the bow. Then he told him to open the east window, the one that faced the direction of his enemies, and shoot an arrow out of it. "'The LORD's arrow of victory, the arrow of victory over Aram!' Elisha declared. 'You will completely destroy the Arameans at Aphek.'"

Next, Elisha told the king to take the remaining arrows and strike the ground. The king struck three times and then stopped. Instead of declaring another victory, Elisha chided the king. "You should have struck the ground five or six times; then you would have defeated Aram and completely destroyed it," he said. "But now you will defeat it only three times." Commentators say that Jehoash should have known what was going on. The way Elisha placed his hands over Jehoash's, his statement about the arrow of victory—it was all clearly symbolic action. The king should have recognized this. The biblical writer seems to agree. There are no mitigating explanations for the king's negligence. Only the curt report, "Elisha died and was buried" (v. 20). Foolish king, things could have been a lot better for you. Now it's too late.

Of course, we know from the start that there was a problem with this king. Before the narrator tells us the king's story, he tells us that Jehoash did evil in the Lord's sight and followed in the sins of his ancestor Jeroboam. Jehoash showed outward respect to Elisha. He seemed to think he could help. Yet, somehow, Jehoash missed the point. He struck three times and decided that it was good enough. I know I am not supposed to be on his side. He was a bad king. But I still find myself wanting to object. "How was he supposed to know?" I want to say. "You're really going to penalize him because he shot three arrows instead of five or six?"

The prophet isn't even that specific about how many arrows the king should have deployed. I know exactly how this would go if this had been one of my tests, and I had penalized my students for the wrong answer. "So which is it?" they would ask. "Is five enough? Is six?' Isn't God powerful enough to defeat His enemies on the strength of three arrows? Why isn't it an act of faith to shoot only three arrows? Is it even about arrows?

The answer, of course, is that it isn't about the arrows. It is about faith and missed opportunity. That is why the story is so haunting. I can't shake the fear that if I had been in Jehoash's shoes, I might have got that particular answer wrong on the test just like he did. I wouldn't have struck the ground enough times. Or maybe I would have struck too many. I wonder if I would have missed the point. I wonder if I am missing the point even now. How many opportunities have I squandered because I wasn't paying attention to what God was trying to do right in front of me?

When leaders ask themselves this question, they tend to think in large terms. They worry about the grand opportunity or great task. This can be a trap. We try to move God's agenda forward by miles when He is interested in the next few inches. Missed leadership opportunities are more likely to be much smaller than our great ambitions. That is why we miss them. Perhaps it is the chance to speak a comforting word or enter into a new friendship. They come in the form of brief encounters and inconvenient interruptions. It is the chance to say a kind word, offer a comforting touch, or say an impromptu prayer.

The Danger of Missed Opportunity

The Bible does speak about missed opportunity. There are several notable examples. Moses lost his temper and was told that he would not enter the Land of Promise in his lifetime (Num. 20:12). Barak had a moment of hesitation when Deborah charged him to go after Sisera, and the glory for the victory went to Jael instead (Judg. 4). Jesus wept over Jerusalem, saying, "Jerusalem, Jerusalem, you who kill the prophets and stone those sent to you, how often I have longed to gather your children together, as a hen gathers her chicks under her wings, and you were not willing. Look, your house is left to you desolate. For I tell you, you will not see me again until you say, 'Blessed is he who comes in the name of the Lord'" (Matt. 23:37–39). Likewise, in Matthew 11:20–24, Jesus denounced the towns that had seen His miracles but rejected Him, saying that if the miracles that had been performed in their presence had been witnessed by the notoriously corrupt Old Testament cities of Tyre and Sidon, "they would have repented long ago in sackcloth and ashes." Jesus' words implied that the opportunity for those cities that rejected Him had passed (vv. 22–23). It can be dangerous to miss what God is doing right now.

Paul associates opportunity with time when he warns that we should be careful how we live. We do this by "making the most of every opportunity, because the days are evil" (Eph. 5:16). The Greek text literally says that we are to "buy back the time." Opportunity is by its very nature time-sensitive. It is the fact that the clock is ticking that makes it an opportunity. Although our concerns are often long-term, opportunity typically exists only in the short-term. Opportunity dwells in the middle space between the past and the future. It frequently has long-term effects, but we can take advantage of it only in the here and now. Paul also links opportunity with the will of God. Those who buy up the time do so by understanding what God's will is (Eph. 5:17). Here, Paul is probably not thinking some particular opportunity that is God's will for us to act upon but of the larger framework of what God has revealed in His Word. When God's revealed will converges with time and our circumstances, the result is opportunity. Truth and circumstance together enable us to recognize it.

Ordinary opportunity is something that everyone experiences. But when opportunity arises within the realm of the Spirit, it is transformed into something else. Opportunity turns into a kingdom moment. We might think of a kingdom moment as a divinely orchestrated call to action. In most cases, this sort of thing happens when we are just living our lives. We may not even recognize it as a divinely orchestrated opportunity until after the fact. A chance meeting leads to a casual conversation that later proves to be more important than we realized. We take some small action that feels insignificant to us but has a profound effect on someone else. On our part, it was unsought and unplanned. We are simply living the Christian life. Yet God turns it into something else. In such a case we are not really looking for an opportunity, it is actually God taking the opportunity to do something through us. We are usually shocked when we discover its true significance.

When Opportunity Calls

However, while some opportunities appear quietly and without fanfare, others are accompanied by a call from God or some kind of prompting from the Spirit. Jesus actively sought out those who would be His apostles and disciples. "Come, follow me," Jesus told Peter and Andrew, "and I will send you out to fish for people" (Matt. 4:19). One wonders what they thought of such a job description. They knew fishing, certainly, but what did they think was involved in fishing for people? One thing at least is clear. They understood that this was a call to immediate action: "At once they left their nets and followed him" (Matt. 4:20). This was not an invitation to be a hobbyist but something far more disruptive. It was a call to leave their old life and livelihood behind and to take up with Jesus. Later on, Peter would say of their decision, "We have left everything to follow you!" Jesus in return would reply, "Truly I tell you, at the renewal of all things, when the Son of Man sits on his glorious throne, you who have followed me will also sit on twelve thrones, judging the twelve tribes of Israel. And everyone who has left houses or brothers or sisters or father or mother or wife or children or fields for my sake will receive a hundred times as much and will inherit eternal life" (Matt. 19:27–29).

But Jesus says nothing about this at the beginning. He did not give them a detailed job description or a brochure that outlined their benefits package. They knew they were being called to a different kind of task, but not precisely how different it would be. They did realize that this was an invitation into a special kind of relationship. The changes that came with it were sweeping and the commitment lifelong.

This same scenario was played out repeatedly as Jesus sought disciple after disciple. James and John, who were fishermen like Peter and Andrew, left their father in the boat and immediately followed Jesus (Matt. 4:21–22). Matthew walked away from a lucrative, if morally questionable, position as a tax collector in order to sign up with Jesus (Matt. 9:9). We don't know the specifics about all of the Twelve, but it is safe to assume that their sense of the magnitude of the change that would be required of them was just as great. *Disruptive* may actually be too soft a word to describe it.

Of course, not everyone who was given the opportunity seized upon it, perhaps for this very reason. One actually volunteered without being asked, but Jesus sensed that he did not have a clear idea of what would be expected of Him (Matt. 8:19–20). It is clear that he did not understand what the working conditions would be like. "Foxes have dens and birds have nests, but the Son of Man has no place to lay his head," Jesus warned (Matt. 8:20). Matthew doesn't say how the man responded to this. However, the silence of the text combined with the tone of Jesus' statement suggest that this would-be disciple changed his mind.

Another prospective disciple was called but asked to be permitted to bury his father first. Jesus' reply seems harsh to modern ears: "Follow me, and let the dead bury their own dead" (Matt. 8:22). Seriously, Jesus? The man can't even wait until the funeral is over? Amazingly, the answer is no. The call is so immediate that it takes precedence over his most cherished relationships and most pressing obligations. Elsewhere, Jesus uses even more shocking language to describe the level of devotion He expects from those who respond to His call: "If anyone comes to me and does not hate father and mother, wife and children, brothers and sisters—yes, even their own life—such a person cannot be my disciple. And whoever does not carry their cross and follow me cannot be my disciple" (Luke 14:26–27).

When Jesus spoke of hating our parents, spouses, or children, he was not talking about emotions but allegiance. As New Testament commentator I. Howard Marshall points out, this is the language of renunciation.[7] Jesus expected those who accepted the call to be devoted to Him above every other relationship. As much as His disciples may love their parents, spouse, or children, they must love Christ more. In many cases, devotion to Christ still involves renunciation today. Not everybody will be happy to learn that you are a follower of Jesus. They may try to lay claims upon you that go counter to your commitment. If it sounds as if Jesus demands that you relinquish all the dreams and relationships that are most dear to you, it is because He does. The language that Jesus uses in these verses is hyperbole, but it is not mere poetry. Jesus means what He says.

Opportunities and Disruptions

The circumstances in which these invitations to discipleship were given and the extreme language that Jesus used when they are issued is a blunt reminder to us of how disruptive the opportunity of the immediate can be in our lives. Would Jesus ever expect me to turn my life upside down at a moment's notice? The answer is that He would. Indeed, He often does. Sometimes the disruption is a direct consequence of the call. Like Peter, Andrew, James, and John, the call to follow Christ includes a transfer from one life situation to another. The change may be vocational. We leave the nets behind and enter into service for Christ. Sometimes the change is geographic. To answer the call we must leave friends and family behind. Or the change can be relational. We cannot relate to our friends and family in the same way as we once did. We still love the people but we cannot love the lifestyle and must leave it behind. Most pastors know what this feels like, but the disruption does not end with the initial call to ministry. Pastors who have grown comfortable with one setting may be called to leave a church they love to accept a call to another that is less comfortable or has more problems.

Other changes that come into our lives as a result of our commitment to Christ are more indirect. They are not changes that Christ has pressed upon us but are brought about by the reaction of others. People who used to relate to us as friends no longer feel comfortable with us and drift apart. Even family members may treat us differently.

It is significant that Jesus called Peter, Andrew, James, John, and Matthew when they were engaged in their regular work. Likewise many of the significant ministry opportunities for Jesus and the disciples arose out of ordinary circumstances. An unexpected visit at night leads to the conversion of a key leader (John 3:1–21). A conversation begun while resting at a well turns into an evangelistic event for an entire village (John 4:1–42). Most ministry does not consist of great events but of ordinary tasks. "Pastoral work consists of modest, daily, assigned work," Eugene Peterson observed. "Most pastoral work involves routines similar to cleaning out the barn, mucking out the stalls, spreading manure, pulling weeds."[8]

The opportunity of the immediate is also the opportunity of the ordinary. This is a common pattern in Scripture. Moses is called while tending the flocks of Jethro. David is watching over his father's sheep. The Bible's theology of the immediate also includes divinely orchestrated "accidents" or "coincidences." Ruth experienced one of these when she "was working in a field belonging to Boaz" (Ruth 2:3). At God's prompting, Gideon and his servant went down to the Midianite camp just as one of the soldiers was telling another a dream that foretold Gideon's victory (Judg. 7:9–15).

Adversity and hardship also are contexts in which we experience the opportunity of the immediate. Job's great suffering took place at the hands of Satan but it was orchestrated by God. He was the one who pointed Job out to Satan (Job 1:8). It is almost as if God had painted a target on Job's back! It was not an accident either. The fact that God set the boundaries for Satan's interactions with Job makes it clear who was in charge (Job 1:12; 2:6). Peter's mother-in-law's fever not only provided an opportunity for her to experience healing, her healing became an opportunity to serve (Matt. 8:14–15). Our troubles may seem random to us, yet Scripture teaches us to look for God's hand in them.

Hardship is common to all people. Church leaders are no exception. They deal with the same trials that everyone else does. Pastors get sick and experience disappointments. Sometimes they have tension in their marriage or problems with their children. But church leaders also experience some forms of suffering that are unique to their calling. In 2 Corinthians 11:23–29, the apostle Paul describes some of the things he suffered as a result of his call to ministry. These included hunger, thirst, exposure to the elements, and danger on land and at sea. In addition, Paul felt "the pressure of [his] concern for all the churches" (v. 28).

Suffering plays a distinctive role in our lives as believers.

James 1:2–3 describes the benefit that hardship brings: "Consider it pure joy, my brothers and sisters, whenever you face trials of many kinds, because you know that the testing of your faith produces perseverance." In other words, every problem that enters my life is an occasion to experience the opportunity of the immediate. In such instances, my experience in the short-term is intended to shape my character for the long-term. These trials are God's Clock of the Long Now, marking out the steps of my pilgrimage toward holiness with each new occurrence. They may make me uncomfortable, perhaps even miserable. But that is not their primary aim. They enable me to keep the present in perspective by reminding me of both my frailty and my destiny. Each occurrence, as unpleasant as it may be, is an opportunity for God to work. But the benefit is not guaranteed. It is possible for me to squander this opportunity, just as it is with so many others. "Let perseverance finish its work so that you may be mature and complete, not lacking anything," James 1:4 warns.

This is an important caution. Not only because it implies that an occasion of suffering can be a missed opportunity, but because it shows what the aim of these trials really is. They are here to add rather than to take away from my life. It may be tempting for leaders to view their trials as obstacles to their own goals as plans, rather than seeing them as instruments used by God to shape their character.

The basic command in James 1:2 is not to suffer but to consider. We don't need to be commanded to suffer when we face trials of many kinds, because the suffering will come naturally with the experience. Pastors and church leaders experience the same garden-variety types of suffering that afflict everyone else. In addition, like the apostle Paul, we face unique trials that are associated with the ministry. These include the burden of care for the flock, opposition from some in the church who do not share our philosophy or vision for ministry, and sometimes opposition from those who are enemies of the church. When these trials come, they bring suffering with them. In many respects, suffering *is* the trial. The command in these verses is to use suffering as an opportunity to add perseverance to our toolbox and then to let perseverance finish its work. The goal is not suffering but maturity. God's aim in it all is to make us everything that He intends us to be.

We Need the Wisdom of Others

It may sound as if our response to the opportunity of the immediate is instinctive. Things come up suddenly and we automatically recognize that it is the hand of God. Not only do we recognize that it is God's hand, but we know exactly how we are to respond. Even in suffering, we respond, almost as a matter of course, with patience and grace. We know just what to do. This, of course, is not true. Our own history should show us that such a picture is a lie. Often when the opportunity of the immediate presents itself, we are at a loss to know what to do. We know something significant is taking place but we don't know exactly what it is. We require wisdom from God, which usually comes to us in the form of counsel from someone wiser than we are, before we are able to recognize the opportunity that has been placed before us.

The Old Testament case of Esther is a good example of this. When the Persian king alienated his wife and permanently banished her from his presence, Esther was unexpectedly elevated to the role of queen. She was extremely vulnerable—both as a woman and especially as a member of the Jewish people. When one of the king's trusted officials targeted her cousin Mordecai along with all the Jewish people in the Persian Empire for destruction, Esther's newfound status suddenly thrust her into a new role as their potential deliverer. At first, Esther was reluctant to act in this capacity, aware of her vulnerable position. Taking the initiative to approach the king about the matter might put her life in danger. Although there was an opportunity before her, it came with serious risk. Esther needed Mordecai's blunt counsel to see beyond the threat. "Do not think that because you are in the king's house you alone of all the Jews will escape," Mordecai warned according to Esther 4:12–14. "For if you remain silent at this time, relief and deliverance for the Jews will arise from another place, but you and your father's family will perish. And who knows but that you have come to your royal position for such a time as this?"

Mordecai's advice to Esther sheds important light on the nature of this kind of opportunity. For one thing, it indicates that opportunity is tentative. Opportunity presents a possibility but does not come with a guarantee that we will act upon its invitation. We must respond to the opportunity if we hope to obtain the result. Esther was strategically positioned to seize the opportunity but that did not make her indispensable. If she had refused, deliverance would arise from some other quarter. Esther would lose not only the opportunity but in this situation her life.

In addition, Mordecai's counsel shows that there is always an element of risk when it comes to opportunity. He suggested that Esther had been thrust into these circumstances precisely for this purpose. Yet he hedged his statement by using language that implied a measure of uncertainty: "Who knows but that you have come to your royal position for such a time as this?" The weight of the statement, of course, is on the side of possibility. It was meant to motivate Esther to take action, not to frighten her. After all, what else could explain her surprising rise to prominence? Yet the ambiguity in Mordecai's statement was real. It was his way of validating the fear that Esther felt. Furthermore, Esther herself recognized that the ambiguity of his words was real. We know this based on her response.

Esther's response to Mordecai had two aspects. First, Esther asked all the Jewish people to fast. In the Old Testament, fasting is usually connected with prayer. It was part of an appeal to God, especially in times of trouble. Having been made aware of the opportunity by Mordecai, Esther acted immediately but not rashly. She did not rush into the king's presence and demand that he intervene. She addressed the uncertainty of the situation in faith by seeking God's help. Second, Esther stated her resolve in terms that indicate that she was willing to accept the risk involved and trust

God for the outcome. "I will go to the king, even though it is against the law," she declares. "And if I perish, I perish" (Est. 4:16). Do not confuse Esther's resolve with fatalism. It is something else. This is faith in its boldest form. Esther's words evince her confidence in God. She has taken Mordecai's counsel to heart. God can and will deliver His people, whether she is successful in her attempt or not. She knows that her future, like that of her people, is in God's hands.

Esther's story is especially helpful because it shows us that there are times when the best response to immediate opportunity is to wait. Her example is of particular value to pastors who, like Esther, are often working in a cultural context that does not reflect their values. While Esther is a model of someone who isn't afraid to take bold action, she is perhaps more importantly an example of someone who isn't afraid to wait.

We do not always need to act in the moment. It can be tempting for church leaders to knee jerk when responding to problems. We are prone to action and would like to act as soon as possible. We feel pressured to fix things. Some pastors and leaders act like helicopter parents, hovering nearby as they anxiously wait for an opportunity to intervene. Instead, Stephen Woodworth, a pastor and ministry leader with the Evangelical Presbyterian Church, suggests that pastors sometimes need to exercise what he calls the ministry of absence. "In its simplest form, the ministry of absence is the ministerial practice of creating physical space for God to minister to individuals directly, without the aid of pastoral mediators," Woodworth explains.[9] He acknowledges that there are times when it is important for a pastor to be present. In times of emergency, when leaving someone alone might endanger them, or when the need is truly urgent. But there are some people who perceive everything to be urgent. Woodworth suggests that there are times when a pastor's presence might actually hinder the work that God wants to do, and that such times require absence and waiting on the pastor's end.

When the stakes are high, especially when there is personal risk involved, it is a good idea to seek the counsel of someone who is wiser than we are. This is what Esther did. Seeking the counsel of others isn't always easy for church leaders. It can be especially difficult for pastors who are used to being regarded as content experts in spiritual matters. Yet Proverbs 15:22 warns, "Plans fail for lack of counsel, but with many advisers they succeed."

However, we should be wary of treating advisers as oracles. It is unlikely that they will be able to tell us with absolute certainty whether the situation we are facing is a genuine opportunity or not. In many situations in life, the decision, as well as the risk that comes with it, usually belongs to us. We are the ones who must decide whether or not to act. Pastors have the added advantage of working with a team of other leaders. Their decisions often have to be approved by a board of elders or some other group of leaders. But whether we act alone or decide as a group and fail in the attempt, we still have the confidence of knowing that God is at work even in this.

The picture that develops of the opportunity of the immediate from all of this is a comprehensive one. Little, if anything, is left outside its sphere. Every context and experience, whether pleasant or unpleasant, momentous or mundane, is suddenly elevated to a new level of importance. When we understand the opportunity of the immediate, we realize that God may show up at any time, cloaked in the guise of our circumstance, and demand something of us. Better yet, we discover that when God reaches out to us through the opportunity of the immediate, it is because He has something to offer us. Ultimately, what He offers is the experience of Himself.

A famous line from a song by Bob Dylan says, "You don't need a weatherman to know which way the wind blows." That may be true. But sometimes you need a clock to let you know what time it is. Most of the choices we make for the long-term are made in the here and now. Sometimes, those decisions need to be made in very short order. Occasionally, they must be made in a split second. The Bible generally endorses planning. It praises those who make preparations for the future. But the battle is often won in a moment by someone who is able to assess the situation through the eyes of faith. By all means, plan for the future, but expect God to interrupt your plans. He may be offering you the opportunity of the immediate.

Chapter 8

Leading from the Middle Space

My son Drew was looking for a new job after working for the same organization for almost twelve years. He left a company he joined while still in college. When I asked him what he was looking for, he said that he was hoping to find a place that would enable him to grow as a leader. Because of this, one of the questions he asks prospective employers is, "What keeps you up at night?" It is the right question to ask. No matter whether you are leading a church, a company, or your family, all leaders lose sleep. It comes with the territory.

This was true for the apostle Paul. After describing a litany of the things he suffered as an apostle—including beatings, imprisonment, shipwreck, threats of bodily harm, and many other hardships—he mentions the greatest burden of all: "Besides everything else, I face daily the pressure of my concern for all the churches" (2 Cor. 11:28). Anxiety about the churches kept Paul awake at night (v. 27; cf. 2 Cor. 6:5).

What do church leaders like Paul worry about? Well, they worry about a lot of things. They worry about many of the same things everybody else worries about. Will taxes go up? Are the kids doing all right? Does that pain I am feeling in my side mean anything? Church leaders are ordinary people who are subject to the same problems as everybody else. But they have an additional concern. Besides everything else, they daily face the pressure of their concern for the church. Most of the time when church leaders worry about the church, they are worrying about its future. For example, a large study of 14,000 pastors carried out jointly by the Barna Group and Pepperdine University revealed that some were concerned about finances, but a majority worried about finding future leaders for the church. "Most would encourage a young person to pursue ministry as a career, but 7 out of 10 think it's becoming more difficult to identify promising pastoral candidates," the study reported.[1] Sometimes pastors wonder if the church will meet its budget. They go over the attendance figures to ascertain whether the trend is up or down. But mostly, pastors worry about the future. The pastor's vision of the church tends to be skewed toward the future.

A Four-Year Plan

During my first week as a pastor fresh out of seminary, I called a meeting of the church board. This was the first church board meeting that I had ever attended. I wanted to make a good impression, so I spent several hours leading up to the meeting putting together a presentation that outlined my four-year plan for the church. I could have gone longer. I considered presenting a ten-year plan at our first meeting together but was afraid that might seem presumptuous. I figured that four years was good enough for a start. I identified four areas of concentration, made some handouts, and formulated my pitch. I was pretty sure the board would be impressed.

On the night of the meeting, it didn't take long for me to realize that things were not going as I had hoped. Although I was nervous, I tried to exude pastoral authority. Eyebrows went up when I distributed the handouts, but I wasn't sure if that was good or bad. Facial expressions around the table during the presentation ranged from polite patience to bemusement to outright amusement. After I had finished, there was a long pause as the church's elders looked from one to another. Finally, one of them spoke up and said he didn't know why I would include evangelism on my list. They seemed politely affirming but not overly enthusiastic about the rest of the items on my list. They seemed anxious to get to the rest of the items on the chairman's agenda, one of which was to decide what my salary should be.

I was momentarily speechless. I spluttered. How could they not expect evangelism to be one of the goals? We were a small church, so small that the treasurer wasn't always sure there would be enough money to pay the pastor. How would the church grow into the church I hoped it would eventually be unless we planned to do evangelism? I'm afraid I overreacted, more out of defensiveness than righteous indignation. I was a rookie. I wanted to be a success. All the markers of success, at least as I defined it, lay in the future. The board, on the other hand, seemed more interested in the present. The church had a Christmas tree farm on the property; the grass needed mowing and the trees needed to be trimmed. Somebody was in the hospital and needed a visit. The lightbulb by the front door was burned out and nobody had changed it yet. In meeting after meeting, the strategic interests of the future seemed to me to be elbowed out by the banal demands of the present.

Like Paul, I spent many nights awake thinking about the church. Many times it had to do with the conflicts and crises we were facing in the present. But just as often I lay awake imagining the future. It's not surprising. Leadership seems incompatible with the practice of the present. Most leaders are unhappy with the status quo. The task of leadership seems to be that of guiding the church into the future. After all, isn't that what it means to be a leader? The difference between leading and managing is that leaders focus on the future while managers are concerned mostly with the present. At least, that's what I learned in all the leadership books I read during my doctor of ministry program.

Leaders are supposed cast a vision for the future. They should disrupt the present by shaking up the status quo. Leaders should be risk-takers who aren't afraid to create problems by moving toward a future that seems impossible to reach at the present. A leader's impetus propels the organization toward the future in a way that puts the past squarely behind it and pushes the present to the periphery of its vision. Right?

Leaders Occupy the Middle Space

Not exactly. Leaders actually occupy the middle space between the past and the future. They have an interest in the future, but all of their actions are carried out in the present. Those who lead from this middle space cannot afford to ignore the past. They are beneficiaries of the church's past and curators of its history. A saying attributed to writer and philosopher George Santayana warns, "Those who cannot remember the past are condemned to repeat it." This may be true. But it is equally true that those who fail to understand the past will have difficulty interpreting the present. Much of the leadership task involves addressing the way the past has shaped the present. This is essential for leaders who want to position the church for the future. The present really is the staging point for the future. Leaders cannot fulfill their obligation to either the past or to the future if they dismiss the present.

Leading from the middle space begins with a recognition that the present is where the past and the future intersect. Future-oriented leaders have a tendency to view the present as the graveyard where the past has been laid to rest. It is a landscape covered with monuments and mausoleums. Like all cemeteries, these structures are holy ground. They are also generally uninhabitable. You could live there if you had to, but who would want to? There is too much decay. Too many ghosts. Future-oriented leaders want to close the cemetery and tear down the monuments. Or if they can't tear the monuments down, they can at least break them up and use the remains to build something new.

But what if we have it all wrong? What if the present isn't a graveyard at all but a garden? The present is where the seeds that have been sown in the past bear their fruit. The present is yesterday's future finally come into its own. The present is also a garden where tomorrow's future takes shape. Like any garden, some of the things that are planted in it are perennials. They come up regularly, but we sometimes forget what was planted and where. Others are the opposite. Those seeds have to be sown again and again, if we hope to get the harvest we want. We need to do the groundwork today if we want to get the expected result tomorrow.

Perennial or Occasional?

The perennial issues a congregation faces sometimes come as a surprise, especially to pastors who tend to have a short history with the church. The consequences show up in the present and must be dealt with. If they really are perennial issues they will also show up again in the future. In such cases, leaders not only need to understand the past in order to deal with the present, they also have to decide what steps should be taken now about the future. If you don't want those ugly tulips to come up again, you had better dig up the bulbs.

Not long ago I was in a meeting where the church's leaders were trying to decide whether to go to two services. On the surface, it didn't sound like such a hard decision. Either you do or you don't. It's not rocket science. The decision also seemed to me to be fairly low risk. Suppose the church added another service and nobody came? It wouldn't be the end of the world. Just go back to a single service. However, as the church's leadership team talked about this issue, I realized that it was more complicated than I had initially thought. For one thing, there was history involved. The church had already tried going to two services a few years earlier. It had seemed to work for a while, then the numbers declined. The church's leaders needed to do some digging to understand what had happened. Otherwise, they might make the change only to see the same result occur.

I was probably right in thinking that such an outcome wouldn't be the end of the world. But it would be inconvenient. There was much more involved in the decision to move to two services than merely determining the times when they would begin. Every aspect of the church's Sunday ministry would probably be affected. More people would need to be recruited. There was also a question about the future. The church's leaders had a vision for a certain kind of culture in their Sunday school and children's ministries. Making the wrong decision could create obstacles that would make this impossible. Both the past and the future had to be factored into the decision.

Ultimately, the weight of their choice came to rest on the present. A decision had to be made. They could not wait to see the growth they hoped to achieve before making the choice, because they saw that change as a necessary precursor to growth. They couldn't make a decision based only on what had happened in the past either. At least, not without first determining whether the same factors were still in play. In the end, they decided to add another service based on their sense that this was what the church needed in the here and now.

In other cases, church leaders expect the fruit of congregational ministry to be perennial when it isn't. They expect automatic results without taking time to prepare the conditions. This kind of ministry fruit is not automatic in the life of the church but must be planted anew if the church hopes to benefit. This also requires leadership from the middle space. It is the leader's job to see that the right steps are taken and the proper seeds sown. One of the major tasks of leadership is the important ministry of reminding. "I will always remind you of these things, even though you know them and are firmly established in the truth you now have," Peter says in 2 Peter 1:12. Paul and Jude say essentially the same thing (see Rom. 15:15; 1 Cor. 4:17; 15:1; 2 Tim. 1:6; Titus 3:1; Jude 1:5). We should not confuse practicing the present with amnesia. Remembering is the proper work of the present. Our problem is not that we remember the past but that some of us want to live there.

Seasons and Cycles

Karl Vaters, author and pastor of Cornerstone Christian Fellowship, makes a similar distinction when he talks about

seasons and cycles in congregational life. The chief difference between the two has to do with control. Seasons just
happen. Cycles are produced. "While seasons and cycles are
both ways to describe the rhythms of rising and falling, ebb
and flow, give and take, each of them requires a different
mindset, different methods and different expectations,"
Vaters observes.[2]

Every church experiences seasons. Sometimes the conditions are no longer there for the kind of life or ministry
we once experienced. The change may have to do with time
and circumstances. People move in or out of the area, and
the character of the community changes. Those who attended the church in the past begin to feel out of place. Or
maybe they move out of the community and commute to
the church on Sunday. As they watch their numbers shrink,
they wonder why the seats are no longer filled.

The opposite could also happen. The attendance might
increase so much that members who were there when the
church was smaller long for the days when the church
was smaller and felt more intimate. A new season may be
ushered in by some traumatic event. A beloved pastor dies
or confesses to a moral lapse. The economy takes a dive,
and the budget goes with it, forcing the church to reduce
its staff. "A wise leader takes note of the seasons and helps
the church adapt, adjust, and walk through them together,"
Vaters explains. "We don't try to change them and we refuse
to whine about them—at least in public."[3]

Cycles differ from seasons in that they are created by the
actions of the church or its leaders. Cycles are generated.

Both seasons and cycles can be repeated. But leadership roles differ for each. Leaders respond to seasons. They either initiate or block cycles. Both seasons and cycles can be anticipated, but the leader's role with cycles is proactive, while with seasons it is reactive. Cycles need to be addressed so that changes can be made to keep them from returning in the future. Or if it is a good cycle, to know what we can do to repeat it. The two can sometimes overlap: "Even while experiencing a difficult season of losses that are beyond our control, with God's help and a cooperative church spirit we can start a cycle of fellowship, joy and hopefulness."[4]

Sometimes the conditions in the church are no longer conducive to the kind of life or ministry we once experienced. In some cases, the change has to do with time and circumstances. The nature of the community changes as people move out, and the church struggles to maintain its numbers. Or the opposite may happen. The community is growing, and the church's increased attendance also changes its character. The makeup of the community may change so that the church's regular members are in the minority. Some churches are focused on the past, waiting for a golden age that will never return for them.

Seasonal changes can be the result of shift in the church's resources, needs, or priorities. During the nine years that I served as pastor of a small congregation in central Illinois, our church's primary ministry focus had to do with children. We had a strong Sunday school program, well attended midweek children's clubs, and a large vacation Bible school program that usually concluded with a community event. One reason for this was the makeup of our congregation. We had an unusual number of educators in the church. It was also due to the fact that some in the congregation were highly motivated to see this type of ministry succeed. It didn't hurt that we were located in a small town either. There wasn't a lot of competition.

Five years after I left the church, much of this had changed. The church still had a strong Sunday school program, but its midweek children's clubs were not as well attended, and the vacation Bible school program was focused mostly on the church's own children rather than the community. Some of this was due to a change in leadership. A new pastor had come to the church with his own vision for its ministry. Environmental factors also contributed to the change. The church had been forced to relocate its midweek children's club from the school at the center of town to the church building, which was located outside of town. Children could no longer walk there but had to be driven. The church had grown in attendance, and other ministry interests were now competing for attention and resources. Some who had been deeply interested in these ministries were no longer attending the church.

Patterns of Behavior

Many ministries are seasonal in nature. They have a life span. They peak and then decline as others come to the forefront. It can be difficult for a church to let go of a ministry whose season has come and gone. This is especially true if the ministry was successful. Many churches are convinced that the old success will return as long as they keep doing what they used to do. In some cases, they may try to find something or someone to blame for the decline. Maybe we weren't following the same formula. Perhaps we weren't praying enough. Possibly there is sin in the camp. All of these could be true, of course. But in most cases the cause is seasonal. It's just time. The ministry has run its course.

Cycles are usually the result of patterns of behavior. Their effects are easy to identify but the causes may not be. Congregational cycles can be like family cycles. Because we are so embedded in the church's culture, we fail to see the patterns that have created them. For example, some churches seem to have the same problems with their pastor no matter who that pastor is. They are convinced that the problem is just bad luck (or divinely ordained misfortune). The have simply had a string of bad pastors. It's more likely that the problem has to do with the way they relate to their pastors. They are experiencing a kind of self-fulfilling prophecy by relating in an adversarial way, which usually ends badly. The cycle becomes self-reinforcing if it happens more than once. The relationship breaks down because the people expect it to break down. In order to understand cycles, we need to look for causes as well as effects. The effects help us to identify the cycle but usually don't reveal the cause. Most of the time, there are multiple factors that contribute to the cycle.

One of the findings of the Barna study mentioned earlier was that a large percentage of pastors say that it is becoming harder to find mature young Christians who want to be pastors. Is this a season or a cycle? On one hand, it could be a season. Millennials are less involved in church. It's no wonder fewer would express a desire to be a pastor. They do not think that pastors add value to the community.[5] Millennials would rather be entrepreneurs than ministers: "Barna has found in previous research that Millennials are keener than older generations to integrate their personal values into their career, and are more inclined toward risk and entrepreneurship—especially if their business idea can be connected to social good."[6] Is it a season or a cycle?

The fact that it is a matter of demographics seems like a season. But when you compare this with the results from the study regarding those areas of ministry in which pastors are most interested, you discover something interesting. The tasks that pastors feel are most in their wheelhouse are those they carry out from a distance. They feel happiest about preaching and teaching. On the other hand, face-to-face ministries like developing other leaders, discipling believers, and pastoral care were among the lowest in the list of tasks that pastors said they loved. No wonder so many millennials don't see value in pastoral ministry. This might also explain why they see little value in the church.

Strong leadership in the church is not an accident, it is the result of a healthy cycle of discipleship, mentoring, and modeled pastoral care. This was Paul's strategy. "You know how I lived the whole time I was with you, from the first day I came into the province of Asia," he told the Ephesian elders (Acts 20:18). The church's future leaders are being shaped in the present. This is face-to-face work that cannot be done from a distance. The problems we now face in leadership may well be the result of things we have done in the past. The solution for the future church depends in part on what we do now. Responding to seasons and influencing cycles is something we can do only in the present and requires an angle of vision that encompasses both the past and the future. We need to know something about the church's history to determine whether something is a season or cycle. How did we get to the place that we now find ourselves in? How much did we contribute to the current situation? We also need to have an eye on the church's future. What are we aiming for? The problem is diagnosed by considering the past. The solution is framed by considering what we want to see happen in the future. The actual work that is involved in addressing the issue must happen in the present.

NURTURING YOUNG LEADERS

How does the church refresh its store of leaders? It's not rocket science. Leadership development is a function of discipleship. Too often, the church does not begin thinking about where its next generation of leaders will come from until the annual business meeting, when new officers are elected.

Nurturing leaders is relational. This is especially true

when it comes to young leaders. However, some of the differences between millennials and Generation Z mean that a one-size-fits-all approach will probably be unsuccessful. Millennials value transparency and collaboration. Generation Z tends to be more private and likes to work independently. Millennials are idealists, while Generation Z is more pragmatic. However, like millennials, Generation Z prefers face-to-face communication.

This means that leadership development in its early stages looks a lot more like friendship than it does training. Instead of holding a class, take someone out for coffee and begin building a relationship. Make it your goal to develop a spiritual friendship rather than recruit someone for a position. Generational differences will inevitably lead to significant differences in perspective. Approach the task as a learner rather than as a teacher. Seek to understand before you attempt to train. This means that nurturing young leaders is a long-term project. We need to think in terms of years instead of weeks or months.

Corporate Attention to the Present

The important work of attending to the present is something that must be done by groups as well as by individuals. This is the particular work of leaders. They are tasked with the responsibility of holding the community accountable.

The kind of analysis required to do this does not happen without intentionality or without direction. It has to be initiated and overseen by leadership. This analysis must be concrete and focused on specific actions. The army performs after-action reviews for both successes and failures in order to understand what happened and why. Doctors and nurses meet together to analyze what went wrong during an operation when the patient dies. Churches, on the other hand, tend not to engage in self-reflection. They may wonder why things are the way they are but they rarely engage in any kind of formal analysis.

Just as personal ownership of the present begins with a survey of the situational landscape, organizational ownership does the same. Unfortunately, groups can be as prone to denial as individuals. Corporate analysis is more difficult than personal because it involves the perspective of so many people.

For more than two decades, I have asked students to engage in a detailed congregational analysis that involves pastoral staff, congregational leadership, and the church's members. They begin by asking questions about the church's size, style, and characteristics. How large or small is the church? What kind of worship culture does it have? What does the building say about the church to the community? What intentional message does it send through its architecture and design? What unintentional messages? What kind of presence does it have in its geographic location compared to the buildings that are nearby?

Next, they ask questions about the church's demographics

and style. Demographic analysis goes beyond the kind of data that can be mined from the census bureau. If the congregation was a person, what would that individual be like (age, appearance, interests, and so on)? How does this compare to the community in which it is located? What makes the congregation distinctive in a way that sets it apart from other churches in the area or churches of the same style or faith tradition?

The assumption behind these questions is that every church has its own unique personality. One of the most important factors that shapes congregational personality is the church's daily actions. These are the traditions and rules that guide its behavior. All churches share large traditions like baptism and the Lord's Supper. But there are also small traditions, the things we do together that make us who we are. For one church, it might be the meal they share after every service. For another, it could be the fact that they always conclude worship by joining hands and singing "Blest Be the Tie That Binds."

Finally, my students ask questions about rules and values by asking those who participate to compile a list of the five most important unwritten rules that a newcomer to the church must learn in order to fit in. Since it's true that people tend to disagree about what they care most deeply about, they are also asked to say what the church's disagreements in the past ten years suggest is most important to this congregation.

Over the years, I have noticed two important patterns. First, church members and pastors almost always find it difficult to answer these questions with a deep level of self-awareness. They usually resort to clichés and superficial descriptions that would be true of any church. Congregational analysis is hard, especially when it comes to recognizing our differences. We do not like to look at ourselves. The second consistent result is that leaders and members often have very different impressions of the church. Church leaders tend to describe their ideal rather than the reality. Church members are more in touch with things as they really exist but tend to be protective, especially when talking about congregational conflict.

The Danger of Collective Denial

The church is not unusual in its reticence to engage in self-analysis. In an article posted by Harvard Business School, Amy Edmondson and Mark D. Cannon note that most social systems in general are reluctant to examine their failures. Three factors in particular hinder the process. One is the emotional difficulty involved in such reflection. "First, individuals experience negative emotions when examining their own failures, and this can chip away at self-confidence and self-esteem. Most people prefer to put past mistakes behind them rather than revisit and unpack them for greater understanding."[7] A second hindrance is the level of depth and honest reflection that is required for such analysis. The authors note that "conducting an analysis of a failure requires a spirit of inquiry and openness, patience, and a tolerance for ambiguity. However, most managers admire and are rewarded for decisiveness, efficiency, and action rather than for deep reflection and painstaking analysis."[8] The third and perhaps greatest challenge comes from the organization's own bias that blinds it to the very information it seeks: "People tend to be more comfortable attending to evidence that enables them to believe what they want to believe, denying responsibility for failures, and attributing the problem to others or to 'the system.'"[9]

In other words, the great danger in this exercise is that we will see only what we have decided to see in advance. This is as true of the group as it is of the individual. This means that assessing the landscape of the present and taking ownership of it involves more than a method of inquiry. It is a spiritual process that requires insight from the Holy Spirit. What is really needed is a combination of discernment and conviction. It also requires a measure of self-skepticism. We need to challenge the answers we give to our own questions. Probe beneath the obvious, the superficial, and the clichés we use to make ourselves feel better.

We do not reach our goals by ignoring our immediate circumstances but by tending to them. In the context of leadership, practicing the present is an exercise of stewardship. It is a mindset that respects the value of the present and provides appropriate pastoral care for those who inhabit it. Instead of dismissing the present as insignificant to the church's goals, present-minded leaders recognize their strategic location on the time line of God's plan. They curate the legacy of the past and lay a foundation for the future.

A Different Kind of Vision

Why is it that the church's leaders are more interested in the church's future than they are in the present? I suspect that it is because we tend to be idealists. We are highly motivated by our shining vision of the church that could be. We are also ambitious. There is behind our vision a hidden assumption that the condition of the church says something about us. If the church is glorious, we are glorious as well.

Dietrich Bonhoeffer has some sobering words about this kind of vision and its effect on the church. He calls this vision a "wish dream" and says that God's gracious response is to shatter it. "He who loves his dream of a community more than the Christian community itself becomes a destroyer of the latter," Bonhoeffer warns, "even though his personal intentions may be ever so honest and earnest and sacrificial."[10] Leaders who practice the present must have the courage to assess the church as it actually is.

In order to accomplish this, we will need a different kind of vision. Most church leaders find a large vision more captivating than a small one. The rhetoric that surrounds leaders often encourages this. We are told to "expect great things" and "attempt great things." What we really need is a vision for the ordinary. "We pray for the big things and forget to give thanks for the ordinary, small (and yet really not small) gifts," Bonhoeffer notes. "How can God entrust great things to one who will not thankfully receive from Him the little things?"[11]

The reason we have difficulty thanking God for the ordinary present is that we cannot see it. Our attention has been captured by something else. In a way, we have succumbed to a kind of Gnostic vision of the church, which wants to exchange its flesh and blood reality for something else. The church we are dreaming of is a false church. It did not exist in the past. It will not exist in the future. It is certainly not the church of the here and now. Ultimately, it is not a Christian vision. Thomas Long reminds us, "The irony of Christian spiritual life is that it is always and in every way material." Moreover,

> It *is* hassling with these particular people who make up my actual life and being in these relationships and raising these children and picking up this plow and being a good steward of this money and that land and suffering through this loss and rejoicing over these mercies and trying to live in peace with those neighbors and dwelling in this community and dealing with that political tangle and confessing this creed and building up these institutions and seeking in the midst of all this messiness to serve Jesus Christ who did not come as an idea or as a principle or as a spiritual experience but in the middle of the very same material muck and mire and "in the flesh."[12]

The best leaders recognize the value of the middle space. They know our legacy comes from the past. They realize that we are headed for the future. Yet they are content to love and serve the church as it exists in the here and now.

Chapter 9

———●———

Disciplines for Living
in the Present Tense

Years ago, I worked in a bookstore in a shopping mall. One of the sections toward the back was labeled "self-help." It always seemed to be a mess. I suspect that it was because people were usually browsing rather than buying. They leafed through the pages, hoping to find an easy solution to their problem. I'm pretty sure that's not how the authors intended their books to be read, but that's what we want.

We live in an age of life hacks. There are thousands of websites, podcasts, and books that promise to provide us with simple steps that will improve and even transform our lives. Sometimes they even work. Unfortunately, the spiritual life tends to be impervious to hacks. It is not easily reduced to five steps, simple tricks, or quick shortcuts.

When I talk to people about Christian living in the present tense, many of them ask the same question: "That sounds good, but exactly how do you do that?" Living in the present tense is not a methodology so much as it is a way of seeing the world. Still, there are a number of spiritual disciplines and practices that can help us acquire such a point of view. Some are disciplines of abstinence, since they are intended to wean us away from patterns of thinking and acting that crowd out our awareness of the importance of the present. Others are disciplines of engagement, practices we undertake to add a certain perspective or response. They may be venerable, having been practiced by the church for thousands of years, or they can be situational, because they arise out of our modern circumstances.

None of them is a life hack. They will not provide you with a quick fix or substitute for long obedience that is characteristic of a life of discipleship. Nor are they guaranteed. You will not be able to apply them to your life by way of formula. They are not a doctor's prescription. You will need to experiment and discover for yourself which ones work best for you. You will probably find that this will be tied to your season of life and your circumstances. The disciplines that work for you now might not be the same ones that will work for you best later on, while others will be perennial.

Apply Discipline to Time

A good starting point for considering disciplines that will help us to live in the here and now is to identify those disciplines that are related to time. Interestingly, our modern sense of time actually has roots in the church's practice of spiritual disciplines. The distinctive feature of our modern sense of time compared to the ancient world has to do with precision. Time has always been a feature of human experience. Some of the oldest artifacts of human culture that we know of are connected with calculating times and seasons. But the invention of the mechanical clock meant that we were able to mark time with a precision that was impossible to achieve in earlier ages.

You might think that the mechanical clock was an invention of the industrial age, intended to regulate the life of those who produced society's goods, but you would be wrong. "The clock had its origin in the Benedictine monasteries of the twelfth and thirteenth centuries," Neil Postman observed. "The impetus behind the invention was to provide a more or less precise regularity to the routines of the monasteries, which required, among other things, seven periods of devotion during the course of the day."[1]

It is ironic, really. The invention of the mechanical clock was meant to be a tool that would enhance our devotion to God. Its aim was to make the monks who invented it aware of the regular rhythms of the day. We might even say it was designed to help them practice the present. But something unexpected happened. The rising merchant class saw the value of regulated time and embraced the mechanical clock. "The paradox, the surprise, and the wonder are that the clock was invented by men who wanted to devote themselves more rigorously to God; it ended as the technology of greatest use to men who wished to devote themselves to the accumulation of money," Postman explains. "In the eternal struggle between God and Mammon, the clock quite unpredictably favored the latter."[2]

In our case, it is probably not the clock's connection with capitalism that affects us so much as it is its association with productivity. Not only are we highly sensitive to the passing of time because of this, but many of us have a deeply ingrained sense that our time must be productive. Because of this, we are uncomfortable with anything that feels like empty time. It is not the demarcation of time into minutes and hours that is the problem. It isn't even the fact that certain tasks may be assigned to certain hours. It is the rush we are in to make our quota. Our problem is that we have been so focused on completing the task that we cannot enjoy the task itself.

Perhaps the monks had it right after all. Their aim seems to have been to develop a tool that would help people focus on the task at hand. By marking off the hours and seasons with precision, it allowed a monk to be fully anchored in the moment. He could concentrate on prayer without worrying about other things because it was the hour devoted to prayer. During the hours assigned to work, he could focus on his work without feeling that it was somehow unrelated to the other spiritual tasks that were part of his calling. His work was his prayer.

The monks used the structure of the hours to capture the time, and we can do the same. Our problem is not the clock but the way we relate to it. One practical discipline that may help us to reorient ourselves to the present is to use the clock more wisely. Just as the Benedictine monks marked out their day to capture the hours, we can do the same. When we segment our time, we are not segmenting our spiritual lives. The hours marked for prayer are not more sacred than the hours assigned to work or even to play for that matter. Whether we follow a traditional pattern or create one of our own, we are essentially giving ourselves permission to practice the presence of God in whatever we are doing.

The Rule of Saint Benedict assigns hours for prayer, worship, work, and meals. You may want to do the same as a starting point in developing disciplines for living in the present tense. What is your schedule currently like? If you are like most people, it is probably heavily weighted in some areas and not in others. For example, most of it may be taken up with work and recreation, with only a small portion set aside for worship, prayer, or reflection. Assign some of that space to those areas that need your attention. But as you do this, be realistic. For example, if you want to create space for personal prayer and it hasn't been your custom to pray for long periods of time, even half an hour may be too much. Creating space in your calendar will not magically increase your attention span. The reason we mark off the hours is so other distractions will not encroach on our time. This does not mean that we will not be distracted as we attempt to focus on the task at hand. We will need to practice other disciplines to help with that.

Practice Doing Nothing

One of the best disciplines for us may be to learn the art of doing nothing. What I am really talking about here are disciplines that enable us to structure the hours that we have assigned to them for retreat, reflection, and rest. This is dedicated space reserved for activity that we do not usually regard as productive. In a sense, we are doing nothing. However, they may be productive in an entirely different sense. Dallas Willard explained, "Discipline, strictly speaking, is activity carried on to prepare us indirectly for some activity other than itself. We do not practice the piano to practice the piano well, but to play it well."[3] We practice the art of doing nothing so we will be better able to relate to the present in a biblically responsible way when we are doing "something." Solitude, sabbath, and silence are three key disciplines that we can turn to in order to develop the skill of doing nothing.

Solitude is foundational because it forces us to step out of the mainstream of action. Solitude interrupts the normal rhythm of our life and positions us to concentrate on the present moment. In a sense, the practice of solitude forces us to come face to face with the present. We are alone and in the moment. We do not practice solitude because it is wrong to be with others. Solitude is not the normal context for most of us. We spend most of our time in the proximity of other people. We are with our family or our friends. We are interacting with our coworkers. We are worshiping with the church. Our problem is not that we are with other people but that we need some kind of dedicated space in our lives that will enable us to face the present head-on and learn to be comfortable in its presence.

WHEN SOLITUDE IS IMPOSSIBLE

Solitude is a luxury that some of us cannot afford. Some of us have elderly parents or infirm family members living with us who depend on our presence. What should we do when solitude is impossible?

- Remember that there is nothing magical about solitude. It is simply an environment. It can have value as a refuge from many of the distractions that get in the way of practicing the present, but it is not always a prerequisite. When solitude is impossible, look for a comfortable space where the possibility that you will be distracted is at least reduced, if it cannot be eliminated. This may be a comfortable nook in your favorite room or a familiar chair.

- Take reasonable steps to reduce the possibility of interruption. You might select a time of day when others are more likely to be asleep (early, late, or at nap time). Turn off your digital devices. You might even want to tell those who are in the house that you are going to take some quiet time. Let them know that you are still available if needed but would like some time alone if it's possible.

• Have a plan. This plan should include a reasonable time frame and a focus for your attention. This kind of approach practices the discipline of solitude in short bursts rather than for extended periods. Know how you plan to spend your time, whether in quiet listening, meditation on Scripture, or prayer.

But just how does one go about practicing solitude? In one sense, it's really not complicated. We simply remove ourselves from the presence of other people for a period of time. What makes this a discipline is the fact that we do this intentionally and repeatedly. It isn't necessary to go to extreme measures. A quiet room somewhere comfortable or a walk in the woods might serve the purpose. The important thing is that whatever location you choose should be conducive to privacy. You won't find much solitude if the kids are fighting in the next room or if someone is knocking on your door every few minutes. To practice solitude, you will need to make yourself unavailable. Turn off the phone, shut down your computer, or choose a spot that nobody knows about. Those who are introverts by nature will find that the practice of solitude comes easily to them. Those who are not may find the experience itself too distracting. Some extroverts practice a modified form of solitude by choosing a location where they will be anonymous and unnoticed. They might visit a park or a quiet museum. If you choose this method, you will need to be careful to select a location that will not distract you from the task at hand.

Pastors have additional demands placed on them. Not only do they have the concerns of their family but are expected to be accessible to the entire congregation. Some have the responsibility of overseeing church staff. In order to make solitude a regular practice, most pastors need to make it part of their work structure. One way to do this is to set a designated time and ask the church's office administrator to screen calls and contacts so that only true emergencies are allowed through. However, pastors of small churches may not have anybody to do this for them. In such cases, a pastor might ask the church to respect the time set aside to be alone with the Lord and make contact later. Some pastors I know make it a point to be away from the church building during this time.

Learning to Be Unproductive

So just what is the task? Now that you have found your space, what is supposed to take place in it? In a way, the answer is nothing. You are learning the art of doing nothing, remember? But of course, it is impossible to do nothing. Even when we think we are doing nothing, we are always doing something. We are sitting, standing, or walking. We are breathing, and our hearts are beating. We might be fidgeting. Most of all, we are thinking. We may not be thinking about anything significant, but we are usually thinking about something. Unless, of course, we are sleeping. Even then we are doing something.

The task in solitude is to practice sabbath. Notice that I am deliberately using the term in its lowercase sense. I am not talking about the biblical observance of the seventh day that was prescribed by the Mosaic law. Nor am I necessarily talking about the weekly observance of a formal day of rest or even of worship on Sunday. In this instance, what I mean by *sabbath* is an intentional and structured effort to be unproductive. It sounds like a contradiction, I know. How do you make an effort to be unproductive? It sounds like work. For many of us it *is* work in the sense that this does not come easily to us. We must intentionally cease from our normal productive activity. We aren't using solitude to catch up on our paperwork or our reading. On other occasions, doing such a thing might be perfectly fine. In this instance, however, we've sought out a place of solitude to learn to do nothing.

Another word to describe what we are trying to do is *rest*. The aim is to cease from ordinary activity, which usually serves as a means to an end, and instead engage in something that is an end in itself. The goal is to stop for a time and let the world roll on without us. The word that Josef Pieper uses to characterize such activity is *leisure*. By this, he does not mean the same thing that we often mean when we talk about leisure. This is not a hobby. It is not a day off. Instead, it is an activity that does not need something else to justify its practice. It does not need to produce anything or create a result.[4]

This sort of reflection does not happen automatically. It is doubtful that it can occur without solitude. It is also unlikely that we can engage in this kind of contemplative reflection without silence. Silence is a rare commodity in our world. To some extent, it is impossible to find, unless we achieve it by artificial means. There are always sounds around us. Even in solitude, we may hear the distant hum of traffic or the quiet rhythm of our breathing. Stephen H. Webb points out that silence is not a natural state and escaping silence is an elusive goal. "If we try to hear silence, we will always hear something making noise instead. Silence, in other words, cannot be the object of an intentional activity," Webb explains. "The only way to draw silence near is to let go of all intentional activity, but even then there is a good case to be made that silence is never experienced in its pure state."[5]

Selective Listening

Perhaps the discipline has been misnamed. It is not a discipline of silence so much as it is the discipline of selective listening. Our problem is that most of us employ noise as a shield, creating a wall of sound that will block out the world around us. We use noise to detach ourselves from our surroundings and often from the people who are in them. We may even employ sound to build a barrier in the hope that it will protect our sense of God's presence. If we are uncomfortable in solitude, the combination of solitude and silence can be overpowering.

THE NEW WALL OF SOUND

In the 1960s, music producer Phil Spector developed an approach to making records known as the "wall of sound." Today, we are creating our own walls of sound as we rely on noise to comfort and shield us. Whether it is the headphones we use to block out our surroundings as we walk along the street or the constant babble of talk radio that we listen to as we drive in the car, we are relying on noise to serve as both a barricade and a point of connection.

Some of this noise is environmental and beyond our control. But much of it is of our own making. According to a study done by the Institute for Communication Technology Management at the USC Marshall School of Business, the average American is exposed to more than fifteen hours of digital media per day.[6] The solution, of course, is simple. Turn it off. But for most of us, this easy step is hard to take.

Here are a few suggestions that may help:

- Create digital free zones in your life. You might make one of the rooms in your home a quiet zone. No television. No computer. No cellphones.

- Combine this with set times when you engage in a digital fast. Suspend your social media accounts for a set time (hours, days, weeks, or even months).

- Instead of being at the constant beck and call of the bell that signals that you have a new message, turn the notification feature of your phone off and set a time when you will respond.

Silence, Dallas Willard observes, strips away the barriers we have thrown up to shield us from the reality of our own life. "It reminds us of death, which will cut us off from this world and leave only us and God. And in that quiet, what if there turns out to be very little to 'just us and God'?" Willard writes. "Think what it says about the inward emptiness of our lives if we must always turn on the tape player or radio to make sure something is happening around us?"[7] Yet this is partly what we are attempting to confront when we experience silence—not only to shatter our denial about the condition of our lives, but to discover that our lives are not as empty as we thought. Although His presence has been obscured by all the background noise, God has been there all along.

Finding that silent space may take some effort. You may have to schedule your solitude for a time when everyone else is asleep in the house, perhaps early in the morning or late at night. You will probably also need to be realistic in your estimate of how much time you will want to spend in solitude and silence. It is better to start small than to begin with a marathon session. If you are overly ambitious in the beginning, you are likely to become discouraged. You will certainly be bored. Start with five minutes and slowly increase it with subsequent attempts until you feel comfortable with the experience. The benefit in repeated practice is not in the volume of your effort. This is not a contest and you aren't trying to earn points.

Despite these cautions, we should not think that this discipline of rest is a morose exercise in brooding. The habitual practice of sabbath in the sense that I am describing obviously has its roots in the biblical idea of Sabbath. The Sabbath has a bad name because of the way it has often been portrayed in literature and perhaps even because of the example of some who have tried to observe it. Whether it is deserved, the popular perception of a day of rest is a drab image of Puritan reserve that has been shaped more by what we cannot do than what we can. This is the wrong picture. "The Sabbath is a bride, and its celebration is like a wedding."[8]

It's also important to remember that the discipline of reflecting on the reality of God's immediate presence doesn't actually require a dedicated time of either solitude or silence. It's not as if these are rules that God has set up for experiencing His presence. They are simply measures that we take for our own benefit because they are helpful in removing distractions. Disciplines enable us to be intentional. But the truth is we can contemplate God's presence in the here and now at any time. It is a good practice to pause on a regular basis to practice the present by taking note of God's presence. Take a moment to become aware of yourself and your surroundings. You are not engaging in analysis but simply noting where you are and what you are feeling. Then make yourself aware of God. You aren't looking for outward evidence of His presence, simply acknowledging what Scripture has told you is true:

> If I go up to the heavens, you are there;
>   if I make my bed in the depths, you are there.
> If I rise on the wings of the dawn,
>   if I settle on the far side of the sea,
> even there your hand will guide me,
>   your right hand will hold me fast.
> If I say, "Surely the darkness will hide me
>   and the light become night around me,"
> even the darkness will not be dark to you;
>   the night will shine like the day,
>   for darkness is as light to you.
> (Ps. 139:8–12)

This is an affirmation you can make in the midst of your busy day of meetings or as you puzzle over a difficult passage in Scripture. You can contemplate its reality in the hospital waiting room when you can't think of anything comforting to say. You can even dwell on it during church, as you wait for the song that makes the hair stand up on the back of your neck come to an end. The practice of these disciplines does not make God present. We practice them to learn that He is *already* present.

Disciplines for living in the present tense do not have to be solitary. There are some disciplines that we may want to practice when we are with people. The practice of keeping silent can be a helpful discipline for reorienting ourselves to the present. It can be especially valuable for pastors and leaders who are tempted to always speak up. The practice of keeping silent is not quite the same as being in a place of silence. It involves a decision to refrain, as much as possible, from speaking.

Speaking is not necessarily wrong. The church and its leaders are oriented toward proclamation. We are actually commanded to speak to one another (Eph. 5:19). Pastors in particular are called to preach and teach (Eph. 4:11; 1 Tim. 3:2). Unfortunately, as a result of our penchant for speaking, our capacity to be "quick to listen, slow to speak and slow to become angry" suffers (James 1:19). Often when we are silent, our minds are not fixed on the moment at all or even on what the other person is saying, but we have rushed ahead in the conversation to formulate a response. Those who hope to live in the present tense need to become adept at the skill of true listening. Perhaps it would be better to call this the discipline of listening rather than the discipline of silence.

But exactly how do we practice the discipline of listening? It's not rocket science. We simply make a determination to let others speak first. We resist the temptation to have the last word. Church leaders often feel that they should have the final say in matters. Don't take control of conversation. Don't interrupt. If a question is asked, let someone else answer it if possible. In a group deliberation, let others have the last word. If we practice this discipline we will soon discover how difficult it is. We will see how often we use our words to try to control the situation. This is especially true of church leaders when they are in group settings. When we practice the discipline of listening, we also realize how often we rely upon our own words to manage the situation instead of relying upon God or trusting that God has given gifts of wisdom to others. We are so aware of ourselves and our disagreements with others that we are not aware of God at all. When we choose to be silent, we find that God is able to manage things without our help. The things that we anxiously want to say are suddenly on the lips of someone else. Those who have not been permitted to speak, because we usually control the floor, now express themselves. We are surprised at how much is added to the discussion by their perspective. We may even be jealous. Even this is good, because it shows that our agenda often includes more than furthering God's interests. We are advancing our own program as well.

What Practicing the Present Isn't

Living in the present tense does not mean that we must always be passive. But disciplines that require us to adopt a passive relation to those around us can often help better orient us to the present. Disciplines like sacrifice and submission compel us to step back and allow others to have the floor. They interrupt the forward motion of our own desires and efforts by forcing us to wait and respond. Disciplines like prayer and practicing the presence of God orient us to the reality of God Himself.

In all of this, we are really just trying to detach ourselves for a time from the slipstream created by the forward motion of ordinary life in order to engage in contemplative reflection. We are not trying to make progress or produce something of value. We are certainly not trying to earn points with God or do penance. We have come to receive. The only item on the agenda is to rest for a time upon the "still point" of the present while in the presence of God. But a discipline is temporary and is not meant to be a way of life. Disciplines introduce an intentional imbalance into our experience by emphasizing one practice to the exclusion of others.

It is like the weight lifter who repeatedly works one region of the body to the exclusion of others. The benefit comes when we reenter the flow of ordinary life. In other words, the benefit comes from engaging in what Eugene Peterson called "the practice of living in what God has done and is doing."[9] This is the art of living in the here and now.

Those who live in the here and now do not ignore the past. They realize that the circumstances in which they now find themselves are the result of seeds that have already been sown. We have sown some seeds ourselves. Some were sown by others. Some may even have been planted by the enemy. But over all this is the work of "God, who makes things grow" (1 Cor. 3:7).

Those who live in the here and now do not avoid the future either. They recognize that there is a harvest yet to come. Our lives are tending toward something. The main task of the here and now is the all-important work of cultivation, the spiritual equivalent to something a farmer does between planting and harvesting. Cultivation involves both rooting out and nurturing. The language that the Bible uses to describe this is "putting off" and "putting on." According to Ephesians 4:22–24, we root out the remnants of our former way of life when we "put off [our] old self, which is being corrupted by its deceitful desires." Meanwhile, we nurture the work that God has begun in us by His Spirit by putting on the new self, which has been "created to be like God in true righteousness and holiness." In a sense, we are making room for a new attitude of mind.

There are both passive and active dimensions to spiritual cultivation. Spiritual cultivation is passive in the sense that renewal is ultimately a work of God. We do not recreate ourselves but must be "made new" through the work of Christ. What Paul describes in Ephesians 2:22–24 should not be confused with turning over a new leaf, positive thinking, or mind over matter. Just as God is the only one who can give physical life, He alone grants spiritual life. The change that Paul envisions in these verses is not inherent in our human nature. We are not merely realizing some inborn human potential when we experience new life in Christ. This is a work of resurrection as dynamic and miraculous as the resurrection of Jesus Christ itself. Indeed, it is a work that is dependent upon Christ's own resurrection (Rom. 8:11; Col. 2:12).

But there is also an active dimension to our experience of spiritual cultivation. The possession of new life is immediate and permanent for those who believe, but its effects are progressive. Our status changes immediately when we first place our faith in Jesus Christ. We are declared forgiven and righteous because of Christ's sacrifice and because the righteousness of Christ has been credited to us as a gift. However, it usually takes our minds a long time to catch up with this new reality. To use computer language, our thinking must be reprogrammed by the Word of God.

But we are not computers. A computer is only a machine and cannot program itself. We are personal beings who are in a relationship with God and possess a will of our own. God alone can give us new life, but we have control over the way we think. This means that the most important discipline we practice in the here and now is the habit of reformatting our thinking so that it accords with God's Word. Reading the Bible is only the beginning. We renew our minds when we express our faith through intentional living. In other words, we choose to act as if we believe that what the Bible says is actually true. For those who put on the new self, ordinary life is the laboratory that proves the validity of God's promises. A renewed mind may begin with the quietness of study but ultimately it is brought to full measure in the rough-and-tumble world of work, family, and church life.

In a way, practicing the present isn't about time so much as it is about relationship. Specifically, it is all about our relationship with God. Viewing the practice of the present only as a set of methods is ultimately destructive because it detaches what we do from our lived relationship with God. The aim when we practice the present is not to learn a bunch of techniques but to learn how to live and relate to God in the here and now. Practicing the present is about living for God by living *with* God in the real world. The best way to practice the present is to look for the reality of God's presence in the dull and sometimes disappointing realities of ordinary circumstances.

Like St. Augustine, Al is scattered in time. He often feels the tug created by the cross pressure of the past and future. For much of his life, Al has been focused on the future. He spent his years in school preparing for a future career, only to conclude soon after he entered it that his choice had been a mistake. He spent the next few decades regretting the direction his life had taken and counting down to retirement. He bought a small home in a beach town intent on moving there permanently. But when Al's mother became ill, his retirement plan was suddenly interrupted. He spent the next several years caring for her. When she died, Al's father's declining health demanded Al do the same for him. Other family members also required his attention. In a way, Al gave up one full-time job only to find another, as a full-time caregiver for members of his family. Throughout this experience, Al found himself brooding about a future that seemed to be slipping away from him. His thinking also dwelt on the past, sometimes nostalgically remembering better days and at other times looking on his life with regret. He replayed events in his mind like an old movie. Every scene raised questions for him, not only about his own choices, but about God's goodness.

Then something changed. Al started to practice the present. This began with an act of faith. Al decided to entrust his past to God and accept His present circumstances as a divine assignment. Instead of feeling trapped, he found a surprising sense of freedom in this. "You know, I haven't had to think much about the future since I retired," Al says with a smile. "Everything has pretty much been decided for me by God. If God suddenly cleared the field for me and I had to make choices, I'm not sure I'd know what to do."

Al is also intentional about practicing the presence. "When I cook dinner for my father, I tell myself, 'You're making this meal for Jesus. You're serving this to Jesus.'" The daily routine of cooking meals and doing the dishes has proven to be a context where he communes with God and experiences His love. Like Brother Lawrence, Al has discovered that God is as real in the kitchen as He is in the sanctuary.

This doesn't mean that Al's regrets have all suddenly disappeared or that he never struggles with his circumstances. Al found it easier to care for his mother than for his father, who doesn't always seem to appreciate what Al has done for him. He has begun to think that he may never have the kind of retirement that he once thought would be his. "You know what?" he says. "If this is what God wants for me, I'm okay with it. This may sound as if Al has resigned himself to his circumstances. But it is something more. He has really surrendered to a relationship with God. "It may be a simple truth but the one thing that the Lord has showed me is something I always knew but has bowled me over now in my life," Al explains. "It is the simple yet profound truth that there is nothing greater that we can do than the Lord's will, even though it may just be cooking a plate of pasta!" Al has traded a past that cannot be changed and a future that may never come to pass for an experience with God in the here and now.

Practicing the present has not changed my circumstances. I am not any less busy than I was before. I still have the same responsibilities. But it is changing me. It has changed the way I think about myself in relation to all the tasks I face. Practicing the present has made me more aware of the reality of God's presence in the ordinary circumstances of my life. We cannot stop the flow of time no matter how hard we try. Indeed, in a way, our sense of the present is itself only an illusion. The world is always in motion, and so is time. We cannot help being carried along as each passing second hurtles us toward the future. Yet if we can learn to be attentive, we will discover the presence of God in this fleeting succession of moments. We are changing, but He is not. We are aging, but He is not. It is not the present that is the still point but God Himself. Even as we are caught in the slipstream of busy lives and of circumstances beyond our control, we are always at rest in Him.

Acknowledgments

Even when a single name is on the cover, every book is a collective work. I am especially grateful to Drew Dyck, Randall Payleitner, and the team at Moody Publishers for their support and enthusiasm for this project. It is a better book than it would have been because of the excellent editorial work of Kevin Emmert. I am grateful too for the advocacy and encouragement I always receive from my literary agent, Mark Sweeney. As always, I am thankful for the encouragement and help of my wife, Jane, who is always my first editor and my most enthusiastic fan. Most of all, I hope that those who read this book will find encouragement through the Holy Spirit and that it will bring glory to God through Jesus Christ.

Notes

Introduction

1. Mary Reeves Davis, "This World Is Not My Home."
2. N. T. Wright, *Surprised by Hope: Rethinking Heaven, the Resurrection, and the Mission of the Church* (New York: HarperOne, 2008), 90.
3. Eugene Peterson, *Christ Plays in Ten Thousand Places* (Grand Rapids, MI: Wm. B. Eerdmans Publishing Co., 2005), 65.
4. Ibid.

Chapter 1: Practicing the Present

1. Augustine, *Confessions* 11.29.39, quoted by Andrea Nightingale, *Once Out of Nature: Augustine on Time and the Body* (Chicago: University of Chicago, 2011), 57.
2. Ibid., 8. Nightingale writes, "As Augustine argues, humans cannot live in the present because their psyches experience time in the mode of distension. But the human body is a natural organism that occupies a place here on earth: it ages and changes in the passing now and will eventually die and enter the food chain."
3. C. S. Lewis, *The Screwtape Letters* (New York: Macmillan, 1961), 68.
4. Ibid.
5. Ibid.
6. Jean Kilbourne, "Jesus Is a Pair of Jeans," *New Internationalist*, September 2006, 12.
7. Richard Maltby, *Popular Culture in the Twentieth Century* (London: Grange, 1994), 10.
8. Robert and Edward Skidelsky, *How Much Is Enough? Money and the Good Life* (New York: Other Press, 2012), 25–26.
9. Neil Postman, *Technopoly: The Surrender of Culture to Technology* (New York: Vintage, 1992), 13.
10. Anthony Bloom, *Beginning to Pray* (Mahwah, NJ: Paulist, 1971), 83.
11. Ibid., 85.
12. Ibid., 84.

13. Ibid.

14. Helmut Thielicke, *Our Heavenly Father: Sermons on the Lord's Prayer*, trans. John Doberstein (New York: Harper, 1960), 60.

15. Richard Lischer, *Open Secrets: A Memoir of Faith and Discovery* (New York: Broadway, 2001), 61.

16. Ibid., 63.

17. Ibid.

Chapter 2: Take No Thought

1. Helmut Thielicke, *Life Can Begin Again* (Philadelphia: Fortress, 1963), 123.

2. Martyn Lloyd-Jones, *Spiritual Depression: Its Causes and Cure* (Grand Rapids, MI: Eerdmans, 1965), 81.

3. C. S. Lewis, *Mere Christianity* (New York: HarperOne, 1980), 141.

4. C. S. Lewis, *The Screwtape Letters* (New York: Macmillan, 1961), 69.

5. Alan Fadling, *An Unhurried Leader: The Lasting Fruit of Daily Influence* (Downers Grove, IL: InterVarsity, 2017), 91.

6. Eugene Peterson, *Under the Unpredictable Plant: An Exploration in Vocational Holiness* (Grand Rapids, MI: Eerdmans, 1992), 23.

7. Rod Dreher, *The Benedict Option: A Strategy for Christians in a Post-Christian Nation* (New York: Sentinel, 2017), 178.

8. Darrell Bock and Greg Forster, "Challenges to the Faith & Work Movement," *DTS Voice*, October 27, 2015, https://voice.dts.edu/tablepodcast/challenges-to-faith-and-work-movement/.

9. Brother Lawrence, *The Practice of the Presence of God* (New York: Walker & Company, 1974), 40.

Chapter 3: Race among the Ruins

1. Joan Didion, *The Year of Magical Thinking* (New York: Vintage, 2003), 3.

2. C. S. Lewis, *A Grief Observed* (New York: HarperCollins, 1961), 10.

3. Stanley Hauerwas, "Should Suffering Be Eliminated?" in *The Hauerwas Reader*, eds. John Berkman and Michael Cartwright (Durham, NC: Duke University Press, 2001), 563.

4. Ibid.

5. Ibid, 564.

6. Helmut Thielicke, *Our Heavenly Father: Sermons on the Lord's Prayer*, trans. John Doberstein (New York: Harper, 1960), 60.

7. Jeremiah Burroughs, *The Rare Jewel of Christian Contentment* (Carlisle, PA: Banner of Truth, 1964), 52.

8. N. T. Wright, *Surprised by Hope: Rethinking Heaven, the Resurrection, and the Mission of the Church* (New York: HarperOne, 2008), 111.

9. Ibid., 116.

10. Thielicke, *Our Heavenly Father*, 60. As a Lutheran pastor, Thielicke employs the phrase "in, with, and under," the same language Martin Luther used to speak of the immediacy of Christ's presence in the Lord's Supper.

Chapter 4: Living on Daily Bread

1. Andrew B. McGowan, *Ancient Christian Worship: Early Church Practices in Social, Historical, and Theological Perspective* (Grand Rapids, MI: Baker Academic, 2014), 26.

2. Wendell Berry, "The Pleasures of Eating," in *The Art of the Commonplace: The Agrarian Essays of Wendell Berry* (Berkeley, CA: Counterpoint, 2002), 321.

3. Ibid.

4. Ibid.

5. Wendell Berry, "Economy and Pleasure," in *What Are People For? Essays by Wendell Berry* (New York: North Point, 1990), 139.

6. James K. A. Smith, *Desiring the Kingdom: Worship, Worldview, and Cultural Formation* (Grand Rapids, MI: Baker, 2009), 83.

7. Helmut Thielicke, *Our Heavenly Father: Sermons on the Lord's Prayer*, trans. John Doberstein (New York: Harper, 1960), 81.

8. Berry, "The Pleasures of Eating," 145.

9. Peter Leithart, "Taste and See that the Lord's Supper Is Good," *Christianity Today*, March 28, 2018, https://www.christianitytoday .com/ct/2018/march-web-only/taste-and-see-lords-supper-maundy-thursday-eucharist.html.

Chapter 5: The Art of Being Self-Conscious

1. Brian Hedges, "Growing into Life," interview by Daniel Darling, *CT Pastors*, August 8, 2014, https://www.christianitytoday.com/pastors/ 2014/august-online-only/brian-hedges-sanctification.html.

2. Martyn Lloyd-Jones, *Spiritual Depression: Its Causes and Cure* (Grand Rapids, MI: Eerdmans, 1965), 17.

3. John Wesley, *The Works of John Wesley*, vol. 8 (New York: J & J Harper, 1827), 393.

4. C. S. Lewis, *The Screwtape Letters* (New York: HarperOne, 1942), 11.

5. Ibid., 12.

6. Lloyd-Jones, *Spiritual Depression*, 17–18.

7. Saint Augustine, *The Confessions of Saint Augustine* (New York: Collier, 1961), 27.

8. Eugene Peterson, *Eat This Book: A Conversation in the Art of Spiritual Reading* (Grand Rapids, MI: Wm. B. Eerdmans Publishing Co., 2006), 112.

9. Josef Pieper, *Happiness and Contemplation* (South Bend, IN: St. Augustine's Press, 1979), 73.

10. Ibid., 73–74.

11. Ibid., 74.

12. Anthony Bloom, *Beginning to Pray* (Mahwah, NJ: Paulist, 1970), 68.

13. Ibid., 81.

14. Pieper, *Happiness and Contemplation*, 75.

15. Pierre Wolff, *May I Hate God?* (New York: Paulist, 1966), 43.

16. Ibid., 44.

Chapter 6: Inspired Intuition

1. Anne Lamott, *Bird by Bird: Some Instructions on Writing and Life* (New York: Anchor, 1994), 110.

2. Ibid., 112.

3. David G. Myers, "The Powers and Perils of Intuition," *Psychology Today*, November/December 2002, 43.

4. Ibid., 43–44.

5. F. F. Bruce, *The Epistle to the Galatians: A Commentary on the Greek Text* (Grand Rapids, MI: Eerdmans, 1982), 245.

6. Myers, "The Powers and Perils of Intuition," 50.

7. Ibid.

8. Eugene Peterson, *Christ Plays in Ten Thousand Places: A Conversation in Spiritual Theology* (Grand Rapids, MI: Eerdmans, 2005), 92.

9. Charles Thornton, *One in Seven Thousand: The Life and Legacy of Samuel Watson Thornton* (Soldotna, AK: T n T Publishers, 2011), http://www.sonton.info/docs/One%20in%20Seven%20Thousand.pdf.

Chapter 7: The Opportunity of the Immediate

1. Danny Hillis, "The Millennium Clock," *Wired*, December 1995, https://www.wired.com/1995/12/the-millennium-clock/.

2. Ibid.

3. Helmut Thielicke, *Christ and the Meaning of Life: Sermons and Meditations* (Cambridge: James Clarke & Co., 1962), 31.

4. Ibid.

5. Ibid.

6. Hillis, "The Millennium Clock."

7. I. Howard Marshall, *The Gospel of Luke: A Commentary on the Greek Text* (Grand Rapids, MI, Eerdmans, 1978), 592.

8. Eugene Peterson, *Under the Unpredictable Plant: An Exploration in Vocational Holiness* (Grand Rapids, MI: Eerdmans, 1994), 16.

9. Stephen L. Woodworth, "The Ministry of Absence," *CT Pastors*, September 4, 2018, https://www.christianitytoday.com/pastors/2018/september-web-exclusives/ministry-of-absence-henri-nouwen.html.

Chapter 8: Leading from the Middle Space

1. The Barna Group, *The State of Pastors: How Today's Faith Leaders Are Navigating Life and Leadership in an Age of Complexity* (Barna Group, 2017), 61.

2. Karl Vaters, "Leading a Church Through Seasons and Cycles—And How to Know the Difference," *CT Pastors*, December 27, 2017, https://www.christianitytoday.com/karl-vaters/2017/december/leading-church-seasons-cycles.html.

3. Ibid.

4. Ibid.

5. The Barna Group, *The State of Pastors*, 119.

6. Ibid., 133.

7. Amy Edmondson and Mark D. Cannon, "The Hard Work of Failure Analysis," Harvard Business School, August 22, 2005, https://hbswk.hbs.edu/item/the-hard-work-of-failure-analysis.

8. Ibid.

9. Ibid.

10. Dietrich Bonhoeffer, *Life Together* (New York: HarperOne, 1954), 27.

11. Ibid., 29.

12. Thomas Long, *Preaching from Memory to Hope* (Louisville, KY: Westminster John Knox, 2009), 96–97.

Chapter 9: Disciplines for Living in the Present Tense

1. Neil Postman, *Technopoly: The Surrender of Culture to Technology* (New York: Vintage, 1993), 14.

2. Ibid., 15.

3. Dallas Willard, *The Spirit of the Disciplines: Understanding How God Changes Lives* (New York: HarperCollins, 1991), 120.

4. Josef Pieper, *Only the Lover Sings: Art and Contemplation* (San Francisco: Ignatius, 1990), 21.

5. Stephen H. Webb, *The Divine Voice: Christian Proclamation and the Theology of Sound* (Grand Rapids, MI: Brazos, 2004), 222.

6. Julie Riggott, "Are We Paying Attention to the Onslaught of Digital Media?" *USC News*, December 5, 2014, https://news.usc.edu/72055/are-we-paying-attention-to-digital-media/.

7. Willard, *The Spirit of the Disciplines*, 163.

8. Abraham Joshua Heschel, *The Sabbath* (New York: Farrar, Strous, and Giroux, 1951), 54.

9. Eugene Peterson, *Christ Plays in Ten Thousand Places: A Conversation in Spiritual Theology* (Grand Rapids, MI: Eerdmans, 2005), 54.

WHAT SOCIAL IDENTITY CAN TEACH US ABOUT CHURCH UNITY

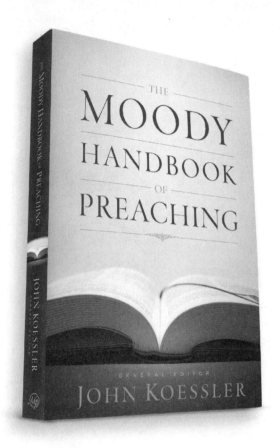